Kirtland's Warbler

Wildlife Management Area

Comprehensive Conservation Plan Approval

Submitted by:

Greg McClellan   9/04/2009

Greg McClellan   Date

Acting Refuge Manager

Concur:

Matthew D. Sprenger   9/9/2009

Matthew D. Sprenger   Date

Refuge Supervisor, Area 2

Thomas C. Worthington   9/9/2009

Thomas C. Worthington   Date

Acting Regional Chief, National Wildlife Refuge System

Approve:

Charles M. Wooley _Charlie Wooley_   9/10/09

Acting Regional Director

Thomas O. Melius   Date

Regional Director

Kirtland's Warbler
National Wildlife Refuge

Comprehensive Conservation Plan

Table of Contents

Figures

Tables

Chapter 1: Introduction and Background

Introduction

By the mid-twentieth century, the Kirtland's Warbler was a bird in trouble. Wildfire, a natural ecological process vital to producing its habitat, had been reduced in frequency and extent, severely reducing the population.

A small, neotropical migrant bird that is a summer native of Michigan, the Kirtland's Warbler relies on a very specific type of fire-dependent forest habitat to thrive.

The situation isn't unique for either bird or habitat. Many native ecosystems of North America have been altered during the last three centuries due to human changes in land use and other factors. In many cases, natural ecological processes such as flooding and wildfire have been controlled or eliminated in favor of human settlement.

Kirtland's Warbler female and nest.
Photo credit: Ron Austing

A survey of Kirtland's Warbler in 1951 found 432 singing male birds. By the 1970s, fewer than 200 singing males were surveyed on an annual basis. In 1967, the species was placed on the Federal Endangered Species list.

Due to concerted management efforts by federal and state agencies, however, beginning in the 1990s the population began to increase. By 2001, the total estimated population of singing male Kirtland's Warblers had reached the recovery objective of over 1,000 singing males and has stayed above this value for seven consecutive years. In 2008, the total estimated population of singing male Kirtland's Warblers in Michigan was 1,791, the greatest number yet recorded.

Kirtland's Warbler Listing Status

The Kirtland's Warbler population has surpassed numeric recovery goals and there has been discussion about removing it from the list of threatened and endangered species. However, prior to delisting, safeguards must be in place that will ensure continued active management for this species. The persistence of the Kirtland's Warbler depends on the dynamic management of jack pine stands, Brown-headed Cowbird control, and monitoring of wintering habitat. The Kirtland's Warbler population would sharply decline without this critical management completed on an annual basis.

Long-term conservation of this species will take the long-term commitment and funding of state and federal agencies that manage nesting habitat for the species. Jack pine management and cowbird control on the nesting grounds alone costs hundreds of thousands of dollars annually. To that end, the Kirtland's Warbler Recovery Team and other partners have proposed the creation of a private endowment fund to ensure management efforts are sustained. The endowment, along with a commitment from state and federal agencies for continued management, may make long-term conservation and delisting of Kirtland's Warbler a reality.

The Kirtland's Warbler nests in young jack pine forest growing on sandy glacial outwash soils. Warblers prefer to nest in jack pine forests that are 80 acres or larger with numerous small (less than 1 acre), grassy openings. This species tends to nest in groups; nests are placed on the ground among grasses or other plants and under limbs of 5-to-16-foot tall jack pine. As jack pine trees mature, upper branches block the sun and the lower branches die; warblers cease to use the area.

The jack pine habitat used by Kirtland's Warbler is also used by a number of other bird species, including Spruce Grouse, Nashville Warbler, Yellow-rumped Warbler, Eastern Towhee, Eastern Bluebird, Black-backed Woodpecker, and Brown Thrasher. Larger openings in jack pine-dominated ecosystems are inhabited by Upland Sandpiper, American Kestrel, and Sharp-tailed Grouse.

Kirtland's Warbler Wildlife Management Area was established in 1980 in response to the need for more land dedicated to the recovery of this species. The U.S. Fish and Wildlife Service (Service) established the wildlife management area, in part, due to the recommendations of the Kirtland's Warbler Recovery Team. The original goal was to acquire 7,500 acres of land on which habitat would be managed for the benefit of Kirtland's Warbler. At present, the area contains 125 separate tracts totaling 6,684 acres (Figure 1). While management for Kirtland's Warbler is paramount, the WMA provides habitat for a diversity of wildlife species, both migratory and non-migratory.

The Kirtland's Warbler WMA does not have a permanent staff. The staff at Seney National Wildlife Refuge (NWR) oversees the WMA and provides limited services on an as-needed basis. These duties include, but are not limited to, administration of timber sales, coordinating with the state on harvestng and replanting efforts, participation in Kirtland's Warber Recovery Team efforts, research, the Kirtland's Warbler census, Brown-headed Cowbird trapping, public education, and on-site law enforcement.

The U.S. Fish and Wildlife Service

Kirtland's Warbler WMA is administered by the U.S. Fish and Wildlife Service, which is the primary federal agency responsible for conserving, protecting, and enhancing the nation's fish and wildlife populations and their habitats. It oversees the enforcement of federal wildlife laws, management and protection of migratory bird populations, restoration of nationally significant fisheries, administration of the Endangered Species Act, and the restoration of wildlife habitat such as wetlands. The Service also manages the National Wildlife Refuge System, which includes the Kirtland's Warbler WMA.

The National Wildlife Refuge System

The Kirtland's Warbler WMA is part of the National Wildlife Refuge System, which was founded in 1903 when President Theodore Roosevelt designated Pelican Island in Florida as a sanctuary for Brown Pelicans. Today, the Refuge System is a network of 550 refuges and wetland management districts covering more than 96 million acres of public lands and waters.

The National Wildlife Refuge System is the world's largest collection of lands specifically managed for fish and wildlife. Overall, it provides habitat for more than 5,000 species of birds, mammals, fish, amphibians, reptiles, and insects. As a result of international treaties for migratory bird conservation and other legislation, such as the Migratory Bird Conservation Act of 1929, many refuges have been established to protect migratory waterfowl and their migratory flyways.

Refuges also play a crucial role in preserving endangered and threatened species. Among the most notable is Aransas NWR in Texas, which provides winter habitat for the highly endangered Whooping Crane. Likewise, the Florida Panther Refuge protects one of the nation's most endangered predators. Refuges also provide unique recreational and educational opportunities for people. When human activities are compatible with wildlife and habitat conservation, they are places where people can enjoy wildlife-dependent recreation such as hunting, fishing, wildlife observation, photography, environmental education, and environmental interpretation. Many refuges have visitor centers, wildlife trails, automobile tours, and environmental education programs. Nationwide, approximately 30 million people visited national wildlife refuges in 2004.

Figure 1: Location of Kirtland's Warbler Wildlife Management Area, Michigan

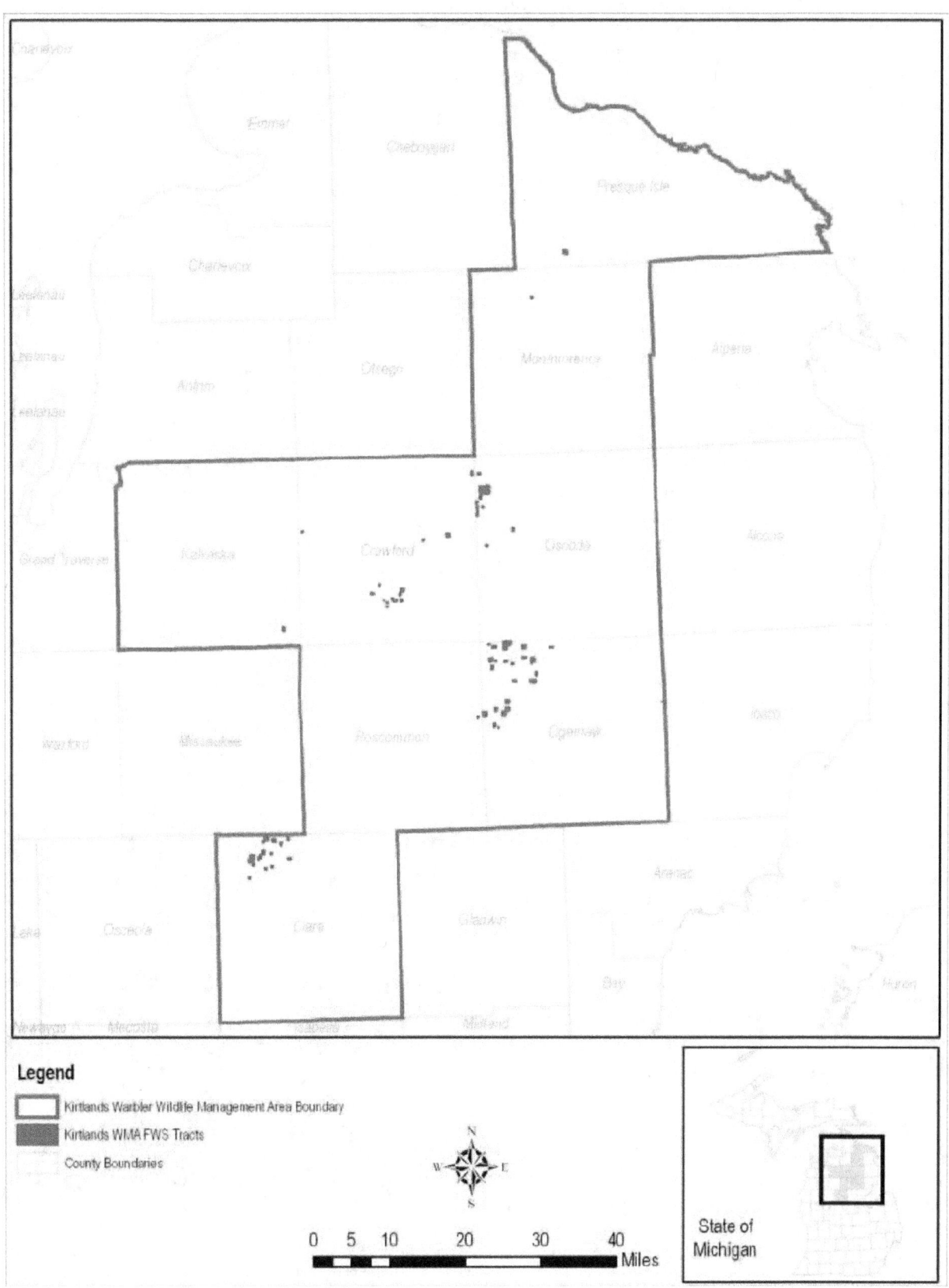

Legend

☐ Kirtlands Warbler Wildlife Management Area Boundary

■ Kirtlands WMA FWS Tracts

County Boundaries

0 5 10   20   30   40
Miles

State of Michigan

The National Wildlife Refuge System Improvement Act of 1997 established several important mandates aimed at making the management of national wildlife refuges more cohesive. The preparation of Comprehensive Conservation Plans (CCPs) is one of those mandates. The legislation directs the Secretary of the Interior to ensure that the mission of the National Wildlife Refuge System and purposes of the individual refuges are carried out. It also requires the Secretary to maintain the biological integrity, diversity, and environmental health of the National Wildlife Refuge System.

The goals of the National Wildlife Refuge System are to:

- Conserve a di versity of fi sh, wildli fe, and plants and their habitats, including species that are endangered or threatened with becoming endangered.

- Develop and maintain a network of habitats for migratory birds, anadromous and interjurisdictional fish, and marine mammal populations that is strategically distributed and carefully managed to meet important life history needs of these species across their ranges.

- Conserve those ecosystems, plant communities, wetlands of national or international significance, and landscapes and seascapes that are unique, rare, declining, or underrepresented in existing protection efforts.

- Provide and enhance opportunities to participate in compatible wildlife-dependent recreation (hunting, fishing, wildlife observation and photography, and environmental education and interpretation).

- Foster understanding and instill appreciation of the diversity and interconnectedness of fish, wildlife, and plants and their habitats.

Michigan's Northern Lower Peninsula Ecoregion

The Northern Lower Peninsula ecoregion encompasses 17,109 square miles and includes all or portions of 25 counties. Landcover in this ecoregion is primarily forest (67 percent) and wetlands (20 percent). Agricultural land use covers 4 percent and urbanization covers approximately 2 percent. The remainder of the landcover consists of open grasslands, sparsely vegetated areas, beaches and rock areas.

This region is characterized by diverse topography with extensive outwash plains and large moraines. The ecoregion remains predominantly forested with northern hardwoods, early successional aspen forest, pine systems, and lowland conifer. Most air masses cross the Great Lakes before entering this ecoregion. As a result, the ecoregion experiences a climate that differs from that of the surrounding continent. Lake-effect snow is common throughout portions of the ecoregion within 20-30 miles of the Great Lakes shoreline. The highest elevations in the Lower Peninsula occur in this ecoregion in the High Plains area. The High Plains, which is also the portion of the ecoregion most distant from the Great Lakes, experiences the most continental climatic conditions within the ecoregion: it has more summer precipitation, the greatest summer and winter temperature extremes, the shortest growing season, and the greatest risk of spring freeze (Denton 1985). The average length of the growing season for this ecoregion is 126 days (Albert 1995).

Retained forest structure in jack pine harvest for Kirtland's Warbler habitat management. U.S. Fish & Wildlife Service photo.

Extensive logging occurred in the latter half of the 19th century, causing major changes in forest composition. Early successional forest types (aspen/ birch forest) are more prevalent today because of past and current management. Fire suppression has resulted in the conversion of many of the barrens systems to closed-canopy forest. Following logging, farming was attempted on a broad range of soil types within the ecoregion. Farming was unsuccessful on most of the sandy soils of the ecoregion, but row crops are grown locally on some of the loamy soils. Some pasturing is also done, especially on the loamy moraines. Orchards and vineyards are numerous along the Lake Michigan shoreline, where microclimatic conditions extend the growing season and reduce frost damage to fruit crops.

Threats to biodiversity in this ecoregion are industrial, residential and recreational development and invasive species, including the spread of established species and the introduction of new species not yet found in the region. Fragmentation, an altered fire regime, non-consumptive recreation, disease, pathogens, parasites, social attitudes and lack of scientific knowledge are additional threats to this ecosystem.

Refuge Purpose

Kirtland's Warbler Wildlife Management Area was established in 1980:

> ... to conserve (A) fish or wildlife which are listed as endangered species or threatened species .... or (B) plants ...16 U.S.C.1534 (Endangered Species Act of 1973)

Refuge Vision

The planning team considered the past vision statements and emerging issues and drafted the following vision statement as the desired future state for the Kirtland's Warbler WMA:

> "The Kirtland's Warbler Wildlife Management Area will be managed to promote jack pine ecosystems that contribute to a sustainable population of Kirtland's Warblers and associated wildlife species. Lands will be actively managed to mimic historic disturbance regimes and resulting structural and compositional attributes, such as dense stands of jack pine with

barren-like openings, snags and coarse woody debris. Research will be encouraged and the public will be invited to learn about the jack pine ecosystem and the wildlife it supports."

Purpose and Need for Plan

This CCP articulates the management direction for Kirtland's Warbler WMA for the next 15 years. Through the development of goals, objectives, and strategies, this CCP describes how the WMA also contributes to the overall mission of the National Wildlife Refuge System. Several legislative mandates within the National Wildlife Refuge System Improvement Act of 1997 have guided the development of this plan. These mandates include:

- Wildlife has first priority in the management of refuges.

- Wildlife-dependent recreation activities, namely hunting, fishing, wildlife observation, wildlife photography, environmental education and interpretation are priority public uses of refuges. We will facilitate these activities when they do not interfere with our ability to fulfill the refuge's purpose or the mission of the Refuge System.

- Other uses of the refuge will only be allowed when determined appropriate and compatible with refuge purposes and mission of the Refuge System.

The plan will guide the management of Kirtland's Warbler WMA by:

- Providing a clear statement of direction for the future management of the WMA.

- Making a strong connection between WMA activities and conservation activities that occur in the surrounding area.

- Providing WMA neighbors, users, and the general public with an understanding of the Service's land acquisition and management actions on and around the WMA.

- Ensuring that WMA actions and programs are consistent with the mandates of the National Wildlife Refuge System.

- Ensuring that WMA management considers federal, state, and county plans.

- Establishing long-term continuity in WMA management.

- Providing a basis for the development of budget requests on the WMA's operational, maintenance, and capital improvement needs.

Scope of the Plan

The goals, objectives and strategies presented in this CCP apply only to the scattered, generally small parcels managed by the Service as the Kirtland's Warbler WMA. However, the Service works closely with the Michigan DNR, the U.S. Forest Service, and other neighboring landowners to ensure appropriate habitat management of larger habitat blocks.

The Kirtland's Warbler WMA was established for the nesting habitat requirements of the endangered Kirtland's Warbler. The habitat needs, protection, and monitoring of the Kirtland's Warbler during wintering and migration are also vital to the survival of the species. Strategies for management of the species outside of the Kirtland's Warbler WMA are beyond the scope of this plan. However, the Kirtland's Warbler Recovery Plan (1985) addresses the needs of the warbler throughout its life cycle.

History of Kirtland's Warbler WMA Establishment and Management

A survey of Kirtland's Warbler in Michigan in 1951 found 432 singing male birds. By the 1970s, fewer than 200 singing males were being surveyed on a yearly basis. Beginning in the 1990s, the population began to increase in response to management that occurred in the 1970s and 1980s through a multi-agency effort. By 2008, the total number of counted singing male Kirtland's Warblers in Michigan was 1,791.

In response to the need for more land dedicated to the recovery of this species, the Service established the Kirtland's Warbler WMA in 1980 due, in part, to the recommendations of the Kirtland's Warbler Recovery Team. The original goal was to acquire 7,500 acres of land on which habitat would be managed for the benefit of Kirtland's Warbler. At present, the area contains 125 separate tracts totaling 6,684 acres.

Legal Context

In addition to the authorizing legislation for establishing the WMA, and the National Wildlife Refuge System Improvement Act of 1997, several federal laws, executive orders, and regulations govern administration of Kirtland's Warbler WMA. Appendix F contains a partial list of the legal mandates that guided the preparation of this plan and those that pertain to WMA management.

Chapter 2: The Planning Process

The CCP for Kirtland's Warbler WMA has been written with input and assistance from citizens, non-governmental organizations (NGOs), and staff from state and local agencies. The participation of these stakeholders is vital and all of their ideas have been valuable in determining the future direction of the WMA.

Internal Agency Scoping

The CCP planning process began in March 2006 with a kickoff meeting between Seney NWR staff and regional planners from the Service's office in St. Paul. The participants in this "internal scoping" exercise reviewed the Kirtland's Warbler WMA vision statements and goals, existing baseline resource data, planning documents and other information. In addition, the group identified a preliminary list of issues, concerns and opportunities facing the WMA that would need to be addressed in the CCP.

A list of required CCP elements such as maps, photos, and GIS data layers was also developed at this meeting and during subsequent e-mail and telephone communications. Concurrently, the group studied federal and state mandates plus applicable local ordinances, regulations, and plans for their relevance to this planning effort. Finally, the group agreed to a process and sequence for obtaining public input and a tentative schedule for completion of the CCP. A Public Involvement Plan was drafted and distributed to participants immediately after the meeting.

Open House Event

Public input was encouraged and obtained using several methods, including hosting an open house, written comments during a public scoping period and personal contacts.

Jack pine harvest. U.S. Fish & Wildlife Service photo.

Initial public scoping for the Kirtland's Warbler WMA began in August 2006 with an open house event held at Kirtland Community College in Roscommon, Michigan. Turn-out was light with four people attending despite widespread notification in area newspapers and in-person contacts. Comment forms were available at the event and made available at the Seney NWR headquarters and Visitor Center during the following weeks.

Those interested in making written comments had until October 2006 to submit them. Comments could be sent by U.S. mail, e-mail, or via the Seney planning website on the Internet. Six comment forms and other written comments were received during the scoping process.

Workshops

On February 21, 2007, members of the Kirtland's Warbler Recovery Team and others met at the Michigan DNR, Gaylord Operations Center, at the Service's request to discuss the CCP and alternatives for future management of the Kirtland's Warbler WMA. Nearly all members of the team attended including additional staff from local DNR offices, several Service field stations, and representatives from the U.S. Forest Service and two universities. The group discussed current management of the widespread land holdings of the Kirtland's Warbler WMA and ideas for more efficient management by all agencies that manage land as Kirtland's Warbler habitat.

On April 10, 2008, a small group met to discuss the possibility of consolidating Kirtland's Warbler WMA lands by exchanging lands with the Michigan DNR and/or the U.S. Forest Service. The group consisted of two to three representatives from each agency. It was agreed that consolidation could increase management efficiency for each agency involved. Criteria for land consolidation were agreed upon and will be discussed in the management section of this document.

Summary of Issues, Concerns and Opportunities

The following list of issues was generated by internal scoping, the public open house event and the workshop. Each issue will be described in more detail in the following chapters of this plan.

Habitat Management

- *Forest M anagement:* How can we change current silvicultural practices to better emulate historic conditions?

- *Fire Management:* How can we restore prescribed fire to Kirtland's Warbler WMA lands?

- *Land Consolidatio n:* Kirtland's W arbler WMA parcels are inholdings within larger Michigan DNR parcels. Administration and habitat management would be more efficient if WMA parcels were consolidated into larger blocks by exchanging for other DNR or U.S. Forest Service lands.

Wildlife Management

- *Brown-headed C owbird M anagement:* Are there ways other than trapping to deal with Brown-headed Cowbirds?

- *Kirtland's Warbler Census:* Will we be able to census birds each year?

- *Delisting:* What can we do from a land management standpoint to facilitate delisting of the species?

- *Biodiversity:* What can be done to improve habitat for native species other than the Kirtland's Warbler?

Public Use

- *Hunting:* Kirtland's Warbler WMA units are open to hunting per state regulations. Some hunting practices are generally not allowed on Refuge System lands such as baiting, construction of blinds, all-terrain vehicle (ATV) use, and using dogs to hunt bears.

- *Environmental Education:* If land exchange/consolidation occurs it would change outreach, interpretation, environmental education, staffing needs and opportunities.

- *Residential De velopment:* R ural housing construction causes direct habitat loss and complicates prescribed burning.

Preparation, Publishing, Finalization and Implementation of the CCP

The Kirtland's Warbler Comprehensive Conservation Plan and Environmental Assessment was prepared by a team from Seney NWR, the Service's Regional Office in Minneapolis and a representative of the Michigan DNR. The CCP/EA was published

Northern Flicker. U.S. Fish & Wildlife Service photo.

in two phases (draft and final) and in accordance with the National Environmental Policy Act (NEPA). The EA (Appendix A) presents a range of alternatives for future management and identifies the preferred alternative, which is also the CCP.

Verbal and written comments received by the Service were incorporated where appropriate. The alternative that was ultimately selected, Alternative 3, became the basis of the ensuing Final CCP. This document then becomes the basis for guiding management on the WMA over the coming 15-year period. It will guide the development of more detailed step-down management plans for specific resource areas, and it will underpin the annual budgeting process through Service-wide allocation databases. Most importantly, it lays out the general approach to managing habitat, wildlife, and people at the Kirtland's Warbler WMA that will direct day-to-day decision-making and actions.

Public Comments on the Draft CCP

The Draft CCP/EA was released for public review on April 3, 2009; the comment period lasted 42 days and ended May 15, 2009. By the conclusion of the comment period we received five written responses by organizations and individuals. In response to these comments we made a number of minor edits to the final document. All respondents who expressed an opinion endorsed the selection of Alternative 3 and the general approach of the proposed future management of the Kirtland's Warbler WMA. We were able to incorporate all of the specific technical and grammatical changes suggested in the written comments. Consequently, we did not produce a formal Response to Comments Appendix for this CCP.

Chapter 3: The Environment

Kirtland's Warbler Wildlife Management Area

Introduction

Kirtland's Warbler WMA was established in 1980 in response to the need for more land dedicated to the recovery of this species. The U.S. Fish and Wildlife Service established the WMA, in part, due to recommendations of the Kirtland's Warbler Recovery Team. The original goal was to acquire 7,500 acres of land on which habitat would be managed for the benefit of Kirtland's Warbler. At present, the area contains 125 separate tracts totaling 6,684 acres. Most of these tracts are located within or adjacent to state forest lands also managed for the Kirtland's Warbler (Figure 2). While management for Kirtland's Warbler is paramount, the WMA provides habitat for a diversity of wildlife species, both migratory and non-migratory.

Climate

Due to its inland location, northern latitude and relatively high elevation, the Kirtland's Warbler WMA is characterized by a relative severe climate. The growing season ranges from 70 to 130 days, with spring freezes common. Extreme temperatures recorded range from minus 50 degrees Fahrenheit to over 105 degrees Fahrenheit. Snowfall is heavy, with up to 140 inches recorded annually in some localities. Average annual precipitation is relatively uniform across the area, between 28 inches and 32 inches (Albert 1995).

Patch-cutting of jack pine to diversify age structure. U.S. Fish & Wildlife Service photo.

Climate Change Impacts

The U.S. Department of the Interior issued an order in January 2001 requiring federal agencies under its direction that have land management responsibilities to consider potential climate change impacts as part of long range planning endeavors.

The increase of carbon dioxide (CO_2) within the earth's atmosphere has been linked to the gradual rise in surface temperature commonly referred to as global warming. In relation to comprehensive conservation planning for national wildlife refuges, carbon sequestration constitutes the primary climate-related impact that refuges can affect in a small way. The U.S. Department of Energy's "Carbon Sequestration Research and Development" defines carbon sequestration as "...the capture and secure storage of carbon that would otherwise be emitted to or remain in the atmosphere."

Figure 2: Conservation Ownership in the Northern Lower Peninsula of Michigan

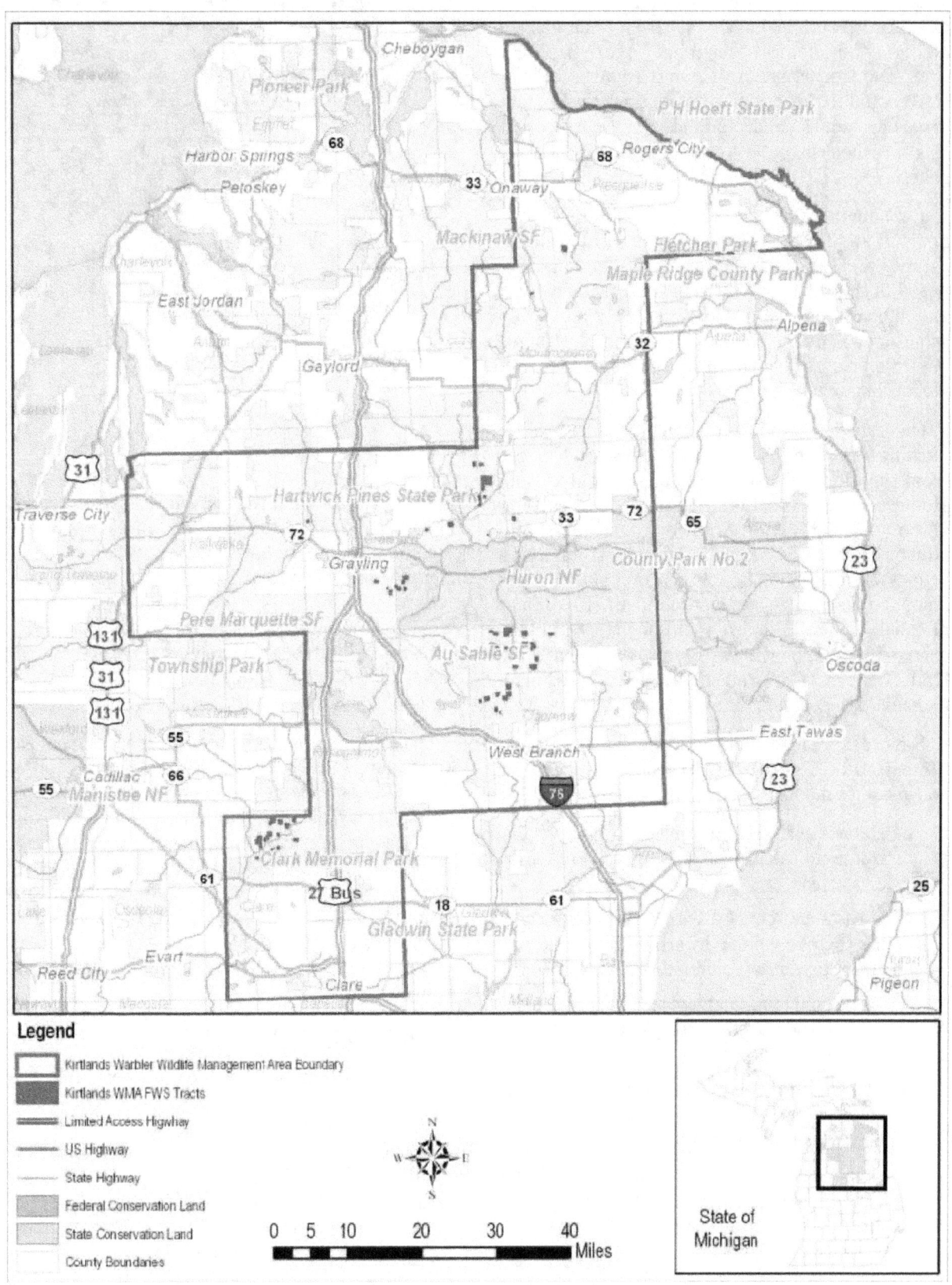

Vegetated land is a tremendous factor in carbon sequestration. Terrestrial biomes of all sorts – grasslands, forests, wetlands, tundra, and desert – are effective both in preventing carbon emission and acting as a biological "scrubber" of atmospheric CO_2. The Department of Energy report's conclusions noted that ecosystem protection is important to carbon sequestration and may reduce or prevent loss of carbon currently stored in the terrestrial biosphere.

Conserving natural habitat for wildlife is the heart of any long-range plan for national wildlife refuges and management areas. The actions proposed in this CCP would conserve or restore land and habitat, and would thus retain existing carbon sequestration on the WMA. This in turn contributes positively to efforts to mitigate human-induced global climate change.

One Service activity in particular – prescribed burning – releases CO_2 directly to the atmosphere from the biomass consumed during combustion. However, there is actually no net loss of carbon, since new vegetation quickly germinates and sprouts to replace the burned-up biomass and sequesters or assimilates an approximately equal amount of carbon as was lost to the air (Boutton et al. 2006). Overall, there should be little or no net change in the amount of carbon sequestered at Kirtland's Warbler WMA from any of the proposed management alternatives.

Several impacts of climate change have been identified that may need to be considered and addressed in the future:

- Habitat available for cold water fish such as trout and salmon in lakes and streams could be reduced.

- Forests may change, with some species shifting their range northward or dying out, and other trees moving in to take their place.

- Ducks and other waterfowl could lose breeding habitat due to stronger and more frequent droughts.

- Changes in the timing of migration and nesting could put some birds out of sync with the life cycles of their prey species.

- Animal and insect species historically found farther south may colonize new areas to the north as winter climatic conditions moderate.

Elk were reintroduced to the northern Lower Peninsula Michigan in 1918. U.S. Fish & Wildlife Service

The managers and resource specialists responsible for the WMA need to be aware of the possibility of change due to global warming. When feasible, documenting long-term vegetation, species, and hydrologic changes should become a part of research and monitoring programs on the WMA. Adjustments in land management direction may be necessary over the course of time to adapt to a changing climate.

The following paragraphs are excerpts from the 2000 report: *Climate Change Impacts on the United States: The Potential Consequences of Climate Variability and Change*, produced by the National Assessment Synthesis Team, an advisory committee chartered under the Federal Advisory Committee Act to help the US Global Change Research Program fulfill its mandate under the Global Change Research Act of 1990. These excerpts are from the section of the report focused upon the eight-state Midwest region.

Observed Climate Trends

Over the 20th century, the northern portion of the Midwest, including the upper Great Lakes, has warmed by almost 4 degrees Fahrenheit (2 degrees Celsius), while the southern portion, along the Ohio River valley, has cooled by about 1 degree Fahrenheit (0.5 degrees Celsius). Annual precipitation has increased, with many of the changes quite substantial, including as much as 10 to 20 percent increases over the 20th century. Much of the precipitation has resulted from an increased rise in the number of days with heavy and very heavy precipitation events. There have been moderate to very large increases in the number of days with excessive moisture in the eastern portion of the Great Lakes basin.

Scenarios of Future Climate

During the 21st century, models project that temperatures will increase throughout the Midwest, and at a greater rate than has been observed in the 20th century. Even over the northern portion of the region, where warming has been the largest, an accelerated warming trend is projected for the 21st century, with temperatures increasing by 5 to 10 degrees Fahrenheit (3 to 6 degrees Celsius). The average minimum temperature is likely to increase as much as 1 to 2 degrees Fahrenheit (0.5 to 1 degree Celsius) more than the maximum temperature. Precipitation is likely to continue its upward trend, at a slightly accelerated rate; 10 to 30 percent increases are projected across much of the region. Despite the increases in precipitation, increases in temperature and other meteorological factors are likely to lead to a substantial increase in evaporation, causing a soil moisture deficit, reduction in lake and river levels, and more drought-like conditions in much of the region. In addition, increases in the proportion of precipitation coming from heavy and extreme precipitation are very likely.

Midwest Key Issues:

1. Reduction in Lake and River Levels

Water levels, supply, quality, and water-based transportation and recreation are all climate-sensitive issues affecting the region. Despite the projected increase in precipitation, increased evaporation due to higher summer air temperatures is likely to lead to reduced levels in the Great Lakes. Of 12 models used to assess this question, 11 suggest significant decreases in lake levels while one suggests a small increase. The total range of the 11 models' projections is less than a one-foot increase to more than a five-foot decrease. A five-foot (1.5- meter) reduction would lead to a 20 to 40 percent reduction in outflow to the St. Lawrence Seaway. Lower lake levels cause reduced hydropower generation downstream, with reductions of up to 15 percent

by 2050. An increase in demand for water across the region at the same time as net flows decrease is of particular concern. There is a possibility of increased national and international tension related to increased pressure for water diversions from the Lakes as demands for water increase. For smaller lakes and rivers, reduced flows are likely to cause water quality issues to become more acute. In addition, the projected increase in very heavy precipitation events will likely lead to increased flash flooding and worsen agricultural and other non-point source pollution as more frequent heavy rains wash pollutants into rivers and lakes. Lower water levels are likely to make water-based transportation more difficult with increases in the costs of navigation of 5 to 40 percent. Some of this increase will likely be offset as reduced ice cover extends the navigation season. Shoreline damage due to high lake levels is likely to decrease 40 to 80 percent due to reduced water levels.

Adaptations: A reduction in lake and river levels would require adaptations such as re-engineering of ship docks and locks for transportation and recreation. If flows decrease while demand increases, international commissions focusing on Great Lakes water issues are likely to become even more important in the future. Improved forecasts and warnings of extreme precipitation events could help reduce some related impacts.

2. Agricultural Shifts

Agriculture is of vital importance to this region, the nation, and the world. It has exhibited a capacity to adapt to moderate differences in growing season climate, and it is likely that agriculture would be able to continue to adapt. With an increase in the length of the growing season, double cropping, the practice of planting a second crop after the first is harvested, is likely to become more prevalent. The CO_2 fertilization effect is likely to enhance plant growth and contribute to generally higher yields. The largest increases are projected to occur in the northern areas of the region, where crop yields are currently temperature limited. However, yields are not likely to increase in all parts of the region. For example, in the southern portions of Indiana and Illinois, corn yields are likely to decline, with 10-20% decreases projected in some locations. Consumers are likely to pay lower prices due to generally increased yields, while most producers are likely to suffer reduced profits due to declining prices. Increased use of pesticides and herbicides are very likely to be required and to present new challenges.

Adaptations: Plant breeding programs can use skilled climate predictions to aid in breeding new varieties for the new growing conditions. Farmers can then choose varieties that are better attuned to the expected climate. It is likely that plant breeders will need to use all the tools of plant breeding, including genetic engineering, in adapting to climate change. Changing planting and harvest dates and planting densities, and using integrated pest management, conservation tillage, and new farm technologies are additional options. There is also the potential for shifting or expanding the area where certain crops are grown if climate conditions become more favorable. Weather conditions during the growing season are the primary factor in year-to-year differences in corn and soybean yields. Droughts and floods result in large yield reductions; severe droughts, like the drought of 1988, cause yield reductions of over 30 percent. Reliable seasonal forecasts are likely to help farmers adjust their practices from year to year to respond to such events.

3. Changes in Semi-natural and Natural Ecosystems

The Upper Midwest has a unique combination of soil and climate that allows for abundant coniferous tree growth. Higher temperatures and increased evaporation will likely reduce boreal forest acreage, and make current forestlands more susceptible to pests and diseases. It is likely that the southern transition zone of the boreal forest will be susceptible to expansion of temperate forests, which in turn will have to compete with other land use pressures. However, warmer weather (coupled with beneficial effects of increased CO2), are likely to lead to an increase in tree growth rates on marginal forestlands that are currently temperature-limited. Most climate models indicate that higher air temperatures will cause greater evaporation and hence reduced soil moisture, a situation conducive to forest fires. As the 21st century progresses, there will be an increased likelihood of greater environmental stress on both decidu-

Bird trap sign at Kirtland's Warbler WMA. U.S. Fish & Wildlife Service photo.

ous and coniferous trees, making them susceptible to disease and pest infestation, likely resulting in increased tree mortality.

As water temperatures in lakes increase, major changes in freshwater ecosystems will very likely occur, such as a shift from cold water fish species, such as trout, to warmer water species, such as bass and catfish. Warmer water is also likely to create an environment more susceptible to invasions by non-native species. Runoff of excess nutrients (such as nitrogen and phosphorus from fertilizer) into lakes and rivers is likely to increase due to the increase in heavy precipitation events. This, coupled with warmer lake temperatures, is likely to stimulate the growth of algae, depleting the water of oxygen to the detriment of other living things. Declining lake levels are likely to cause large impacts to the current distribution of wetlands. There is some chance that some wetlands could gradually migrate, but in areas where their migration is limited by the topography, they would disappear. Changes in bird populations and other native wildlife have already been linked to increasing temperatures and more changes are likely in the future. Wildlife populations are particularly susceptible to climate extremes due to the effects of drought on their food sources.

Figure 3: Jack Pine Habitat Suitability Hot Spots of Current and Modeled Importance Values (A.D. 2100)

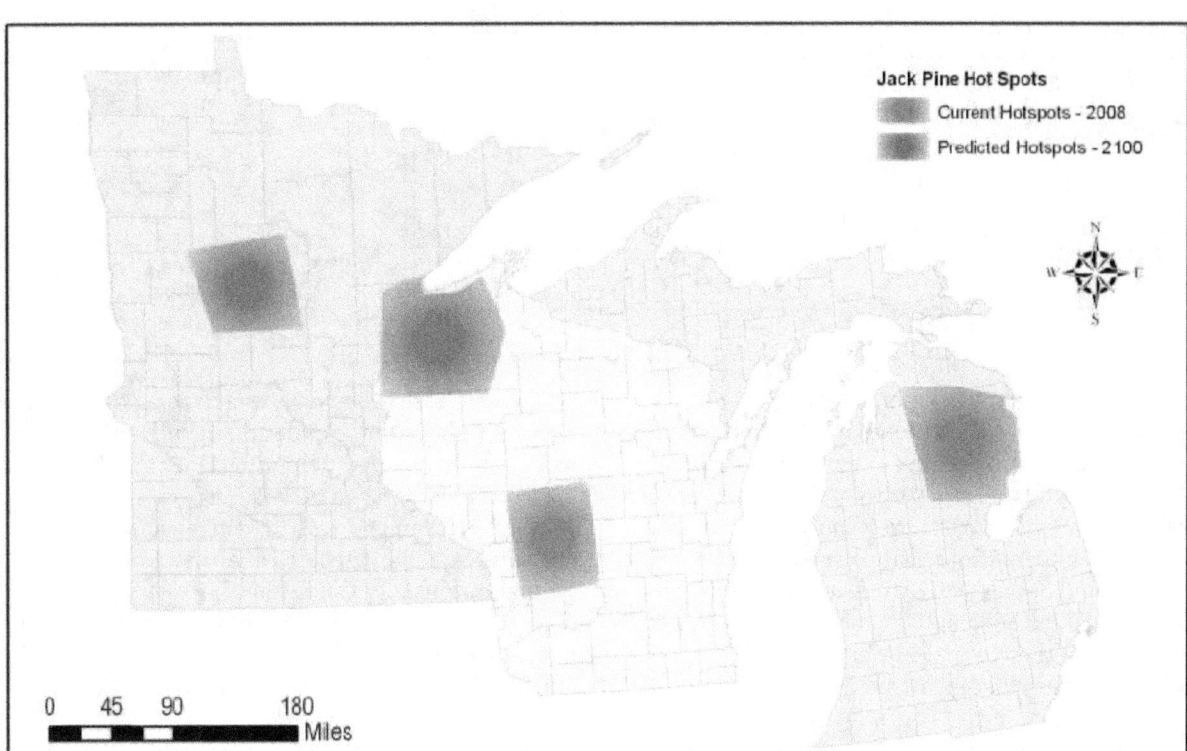

The figure shows hotspot patches of the current and modeled distribution and the average of three. Hot spots are defined as the top 10 percent of importance values (Matthews et al. 2004)

Climate Change Impacts to Kirtland's Warbler Habitat

The predicted climate change scenarios for the Midwest Region include a shift in forested ecosystems as well as hydrologic factors. The future of the Kirtland's Warbler is in a large part tied to the extent and availability of suitable jack pine forests. These forests will likely change in extent over time due to global climate change.

The U.S. Forest Service, Northern Research Center, modeled and mapped 134 tree species from the eastern United States for potential response to several scenarios of climate change (Prasad et al. 2007). The scenarios, built upon three independent climate models, predicted for both low and high intensity CO^2 emissions through the year 2100. The model only depicted potential suitable habitats of species and not actual changes in ranges of the spe-

cies. Factors that influence actual migration of a tree species include fragmentation of landscapes, competition with other species, and other possible inhibiting and accelerating factors. These factors are beyond the scope of the model.

Of the 134 species, approximately 66 species would gain and 54 species would lose at least 10 percent of their suitable habitat under climate change. In general, the results show that species will have a lot less pressure to move to more suitable habitats if lower emission of greenhouse gases occurs. Under the lower emission scenario, jack pine might well persist within its current range although the extent and quality may be reduced by an unknown amount. Under the highest emissions scenario, we may see a greater reduction in the current extent of jack pine in Michigan and a shift in environmental conditions suitable for jack pine growth and development to the west in Wisconsin and Minnesota.

Table 1: Soils of the Kirtland's Warbler WMA

Soil Mapping Units/ Associations	Acres	% of WMA
Grayling- Graycalm- Au Gres	2,286.00	34.7
Rubicon- Grayling- Croswell	2,217	33.7
Grayling- Rubicon- Au Gres	1,340	20.4
Graycalm- Kalkaska- Montcalm	307	4.7
Rubicon- Graycalm- Montcalm	226	3.4
Rubicon- Croswell- Au Gres	202	3.1
Menominee- Markey- Montcalm	4	0.1

The two scenarios, when averaged, show that jack pine will have approximately the same potential habitat value, with some changes in distribution, within the eight-state Midwest Region. Current jack pine forests of the Lower and Upper Peninsula of Michigan, including the Kirtland's Warbler WMA, could decrease in extent and/or quality. However, new areas of potential habitat for jack pine will be found to the west of Michigan in western and north-western Wisconsin and at the prairie-boreal forest transition area in northwest Minnesota (Figure 3).

Several national wildlife refuges and wetland management districts are located in or near these new potential "hotspots." Thus, if climate scenarios play out as predicted, there may be reduction in the current distribution and quality of jack pine forests in Michigan and an expansion in the distribution of suitable environmental conditions for jack pine forests in west Wisconsin and west-central Minnesota. Service lands in these regions that host remnant jack pine stands might allocate some management effort into preserving these trees and hence seed sources. Should conditions for jack pine improve this will provide a basis for future stand development. If the population of Kirtland's Warbler continues to rise, there is greater potential for individuals to disburse into new areas of suitable habitat or serve as source populations for transplants to new habitats.

Geology and Glaciation

Michigan's northern Lower Peninsula is underlain by Paleozoic bedrock and was completely glaciated during the Late Wisconsinan period. The underlying bedrock, which was deposited in marine and near-shore environments, includes sandstone, shale, limestone and dolomite (Dorr and Eschman 1984). Limestone bedrock is locally exposed along the Lake Huron and Lake Michigan shorelines, but the sandy glacial deposits over most of the ecoregion are generally thick; the thickest deposits are 600-1,100 feet near Cadillac and Grayling. Common glacial landforms include lake plain, outwash plain, end moraine and ground moraine.

Soils

The physical characteristics of the Kirtland's Warbler WMA are consistent with most of the northern half of the Lower Peninsula of Michigan. Topographically, the land is flat to gently rolling and landforms are glacially derived. In terms of physiography and land classification, the majority of the stands (94 percent) are in the Highplains Landtype Association with 6 percent in the Presque Isle Landtype Association. Three soil associations dominate the tracts namely Grayling – Graycalm - Au Gres (35 percent), Rubicon – Grayling - Croswell (34 percent), and Grayling – Rubicon - Au Gres (21 percent). All of the soil series in the three soil associations are sands (Goebel et al. 2007). See Table 1.

Surface Hydrology

All of the parcels within the Kirtland's Warbler WMA are located on well-drained upland soils (Table 1). However, the northern Lower Peninsula has a variety of surface waters. Interior open wetlands found within this ecoregion include intermittent wetlands, bogs, northern wet meadows, northern fens, and poor fens. Coastal wetlands include interdunal wetlands, wooded dune and swale complexes, and Great Lakes marshes.

Archeological and Cultural Values

The Service has almost no information about cultural resources (in this case historic and prehistoric archeological sites, buildings and structures, places of historic events or persons, traditional cultural properties including sacred sites, and properties on or eligible for the National Register of Historic Places) within these eight counties of Michigan. For example, some counties have no historic properties on the National Register of Historic Places listed and the total of historic properties in the eight counties is 15. Furthermore, none of the historic properties are archeological sites and none are on or in the vicinity of current Kirtland's Warbler WMA tracts. Even the chronology of prehistoric cultures and historic settlements is absent.

The Service has records of 37 historic period sites, mostly cabin sites, on Service land and no recorded prehistoric sites. A number of 19th and early 20th century logging camps and related logging facilities are expected to be located in the area and if any are on Service land they likely would be considered eligible for the National Register. The Service has no archeological collections from the Kirtland's Warbler WMA.

Social and Economic Context

The eight counties in the Michigan's northern Lower Peninsula that encompass the Kirtland's Warbler WMA are primarily rural in nature. The economy is limited by a lower population, few industries and reduced agriculture compared to southern Michigan. Seasonal and tourism related employment is significant. For example, Ogemaw County is typical of the region and has the most Kirtland's Warbler WMA parcels and acreage. As of the census of 2000, there were 21,645 people, 8,842 households, and 6,189 families residing in the county. The population density was 38 people per square mile (15/km²).

The racial makeup of the county was 97.48 percent White, 0.13 percent Black or African American, 0.60 percent Native American, 0.38 percent Asian, 0.03 percent Pacific Islander, 0.13 percent from other races, and 1.25 percent from two or more races. Just 1.16 percent of the population was Hispanic or Latino of any race and 97.9 percent spoke only English at home.

In the county, the age of the population was spread out with 23.50 percent under 18, 6.40 percent from 18 to 24, 24.40 percent from 25 to 44, 27 percent from 45 to 64, and 18.80 percent who were 65 years of age or older. The median age was 42 years. For every 100 females there were 98.40 males.

The median income for a household in the county was $30,474, and the median income for a family was $34,988. Males had a median income of $31,003 versus $20,544 for females. The per capita income for the county was $15,768. About 11 percent of families and 14 percent of the population were below the poverty line, including 18.50 percent of those under age 18 and 9.90 percent of those age 65 or over (U.S. Census Bureau 2005).

Environmental Contaminants

In national maps, the northern Lower Peninsula of Michigan is not located in an area of high deposition of many substances (pH, Hg, NOx) that are elevated further south and east in the Great Lakes Basin.

Due to remote locations, most Kirtland's Warbler WMA parcels are not near any point-sources of pollution. Therefore, most parcels are not at risk from spills or other releases from facilities. However, at least seven of the parcels are encumbered with oil and gas leases and some may have active wells. The level of oil and gas production is relatively low on these isolated sites. However, petroleum spills are a possibility on any active site.

The landscape is likely to be impacted from air pollution that may originate from other, ore industrialized, areas of the Great Lakes basin and beyond.

Natural Resources

Historic Habitat Conditions

Historical evidence indicates that prior to European settlement pine barrens of the northern Lower Peninsula of Michigan were large, relatively open, xeric tracts with clusters of jack pine and red pine of varying density scattered throughout. Common shrubs and herbaceous plants included cherry, *Amelanchier* spp., sweet fern, and bluestem. Fire, both anthropogenic and other, and biotic factors like jack pine budworm (*Choristoneura pinus*) acted as the primary disturbance mechanisms that maintained these ecosystems and created the diverse pattern of thickly forested conifer stands scattered among openings (Figure 4).

Wildfire History

Fire always has been an important disturbance factor in the jack pine barrens. The young jack pines upon which the Kirtland's Warbler depends for nesting habitat grow after fire removes older trees and rejuvenates the forest. Heat from fire opens jack pine cones to release seeds. Fire also prepares the ground for the germination of the seeds.

Historically, the jack pine barrens were maintained by naturally occurring wildfires that swept through the region. The jack pine held little value for the lumbermen who came in search of white pine. Once logging activity ended in the 1880s, the continuing forest fires helped increase the area of jack pine in the northern Lower Peninsula, creating more potential nesting habitat.

Plant Communities and Habitat Types

Landcover in the northern Lower Peninsula of Michigan is primarily forest (67 percent) and wetlands (20 percent). Agricultural land use covers 4 percent and urbanization covers approximately 2 percent (Figure 5 on page 20). The remainder of the landcover consists of open grasslands, sparsely vegetated areas, beaches and rock areas. This region is characterized by diverse topography with extensive outwash plains and large moraines. The ecoregion remains predominantly forested with northern hardwoods, early successional aspen forest, pine systems, and lowland conifer (Michigan DNR 2005).

Wetlands

Approximately 2 percent of the Kirtland's Warbler WMA, or 137 acres, is characterized by wetland ecosystems and 0.6 percent is classified as lakes. No detailed inventories or research have been conducted within these habitat types, however.

Uplands

According to the assessment of Goebel et al. (2007), 41 percent of the stands (2,695 acres) are between 5-23 years old, while 14 percent (959 acres) are less than 5 years old and 45 percent (2,298 acres) are greater than 23 years old. It is important to note that many of the stands have multiple cohorts; to determine the age of each stand the most extensive cohort was considered indicative of the overall stand age.

Seventeen overstory (stems greater than 4 inches dbh) tree species have been found at Kirtland's Warbler WMA, with jack pine, red pine, scarlet oak, trembling aspen, black cherry, black oak, northern red oak, and bigtooth aspen as common overstory species. Other less common species include eastern white pine, red maple, balsam fir, green ash, black ash, white spruce, northern pin oak and fire cherry

The younger stands are dominated by several species including jack pine, trembling aspen, and black cherry, while the 5-23 year old stands are dominated by jack pine. In some instances, the 5-23 year old stands occur under sparsely distributed canopy of older red pine. The older stands (greater than 23 years old) have variable composition, but for the most part are dominated by mature jack pine.

The understory (stems less than 4 inches dbh and greater than 1 inch dbh) included 23 species, the most frequent being:

- jack pine
- red pine
- white pine
- black cherry
- fire cherry
- white oak
- scarlet oak
- northern pin oak
- northern red oak
- black oak

Figure 4: Pre-European Settlement Cover Typesof the Northern Lower Peninsula, Michigan

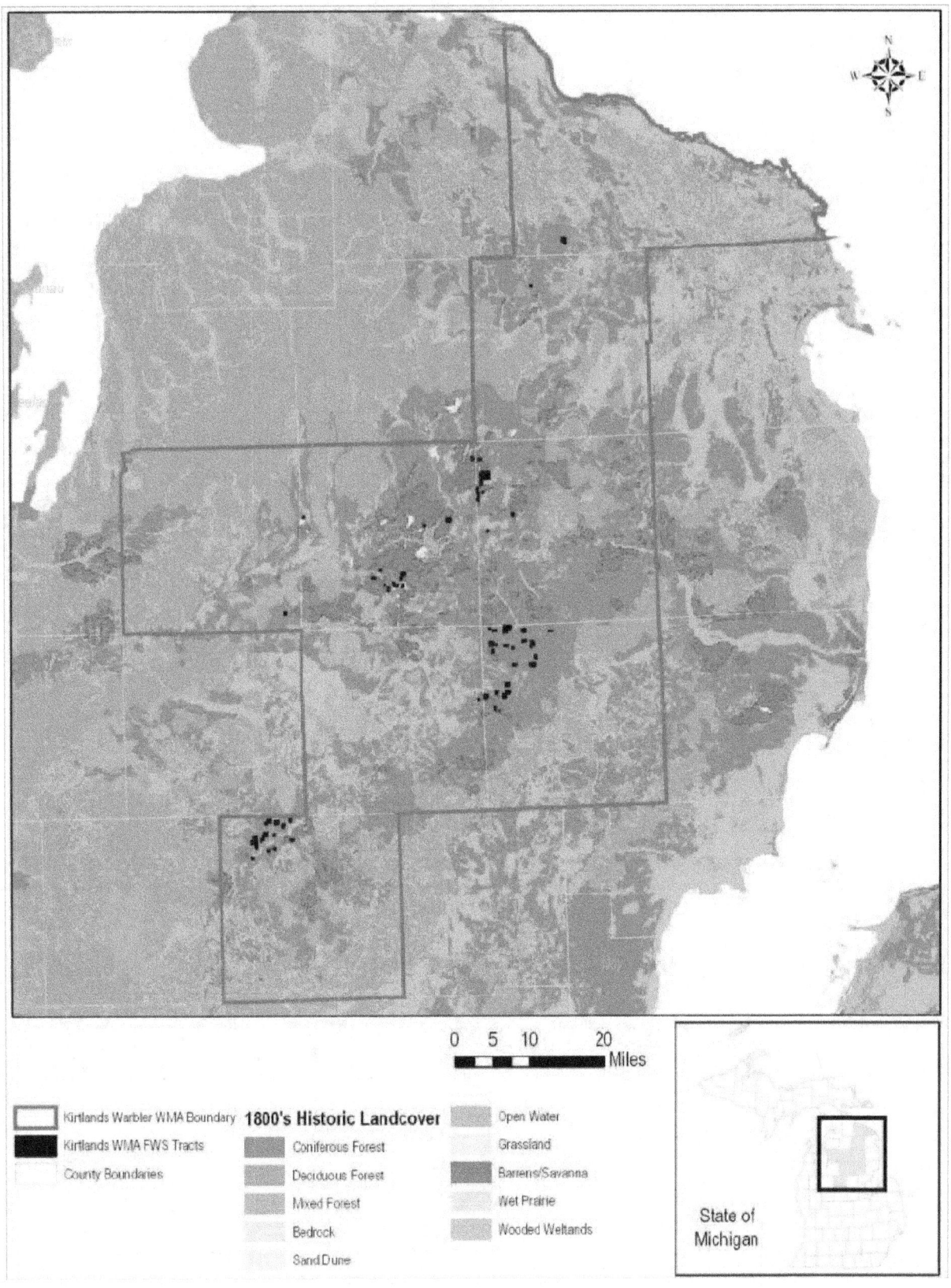

Figure 5: Current Landcover of the Northern Lower Peninsula of Michigan

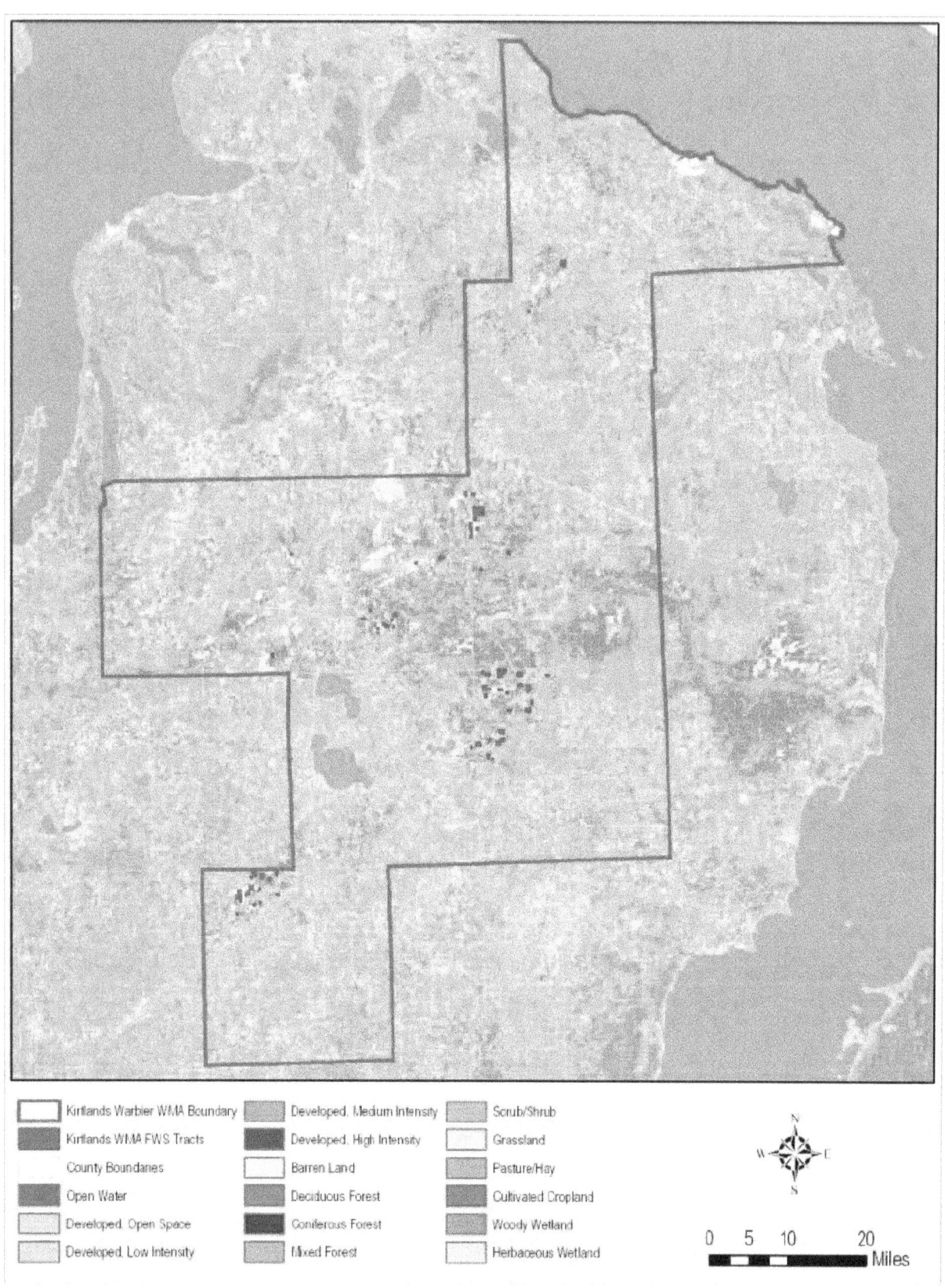

Kirtlands Warbler WMA Boundary	Developed, Medium Intensity	Scrub/Shrub	
Kirtlands WMA FWS Tracts	Developed, High Intensity	Grassland	
County Boundaries	Barren Land	Pasture/Hay	
Open Water	Deciduous Forest	Cultivated Cropland	
Developed, Open Space	Coniferous Forest	Woody Wetland	
Developed, Low Intensity	Mixed Forest	Herbaceous Wetland	

0   5   10   20   Miles

- trembling aspen
- bigtooth aspen

Although present, red maple, green ash, black ash, white ash, balsam fir, white spruce, tag alder, witch-hazel, serviceberry, hawthorn and birch were less common. Jack pine was the most common understory tree sampled and is characteristic of the understory in all three age classes. Black cherry, trembling aspen, and northern red oak are also common but are generally associated with those stands less than 5 years old and 5-23 years old.

The seedling layer (stems less than 1 inch dbh) is characterized by 29 woody plants including:

- jack pine
- red pine
- eastern white pine
- bigtooth aspen
- trembling aspen
- white oak
- scarlet oak
- northern pin oak
- northern red oak
- black oak
- black cherry
- fire cherry
- choke cherry
- red maple
- green ash
- black ash
- American basswood
- balsam fir
- witch-hazel
- serviceberry
- alternate-leaf dogwood
- dogwood
- hawthorne
- eastern hophornbeam
- willow
- honeysuckle
- currant
- gooseberry

Clear cuts with reserves at Kirtland's Warbler WMA. U.S. Fish & Wildlife Service photo.

In terms of stand structure, the primary interest for Kirtland's Warbler management is jack pine stem density. On the Kirtland's Warbler WMA, overstory stem density is highest in the older age class (greater than 23 years old) than the other two younger age classes, while understory stem density tends to be highest on average in the youngest age class (less than 5 years old). There is also considerable variability in overstory and understory stem density within each age group, especially the youngest age class. This trend is largely due to the range of conditions associated with recent harvest activities where portions of the stands may not have been harvested.

Most importantly to Kirtland's Warbler, mean total stem density in the 5 to 23-year-old stands is lower than is optimal. For instance, average total stem density is 73.1 (10.8) stems per acre in the 5 to 23-year-old stands and 333.0 (14.5) stems per acre in the older stands. Similarly, jack pine densities in the 5 to 23-years-old stands have on average 12.5 (5.2) overstory stems per acre and 24.7 (2.5) understory stems per acre for a total average of 37.2 (6.1) jack pine stems per acre (91.8 (15.0) stems ha-1). While these estimates are indicative of under-stocking in these Kirtland's Warbler WMA stands, it is important to point out that the variability within a tract may "depress" these estimates when mean values are calculated. It is also important to realize that overstory and understory density tended to be quite "patchy" in many of the Kirtland's Warbler WMA stands.

As observed in the overstory and understory stem density values, seedling densities are also quite variable within age groups, with an average of 1,779 (n=302) total seedlings ac-1 in the young age class (less than 5 years old), 2,514 (155) seedlings ac-1 in the 5-23 year old class, and 2,804 (209) seedlings ac-1 in the oldest age class (greater than 23 years old). Jack pine seedling densities are considerably lower, comprising less than 25 percent of the total seedling community in all three age classes.

The inventory of Geobel et al. (2007) suggests that none of the stands between 5-23 years old in the Kirtland's Warbler WMA appear to have optimal stocking for breeding Kirtland's Warbler (greater than 1,012 stems ac-1). However, as mentioned previously, it is important to keep in mind that there is considerable variation between stands in terms of seedling density. These results suggest that past regeneration efforts, which appear to vary considerably in terms of the methods used, did not always provide the preferred stocking levels of jack pine for Kirtland's Warbler. In the future, other regeneration methods may be advisable, including direct seeding and the use of prescribed fire.

It is also important to point out that the species composition and structure (including age structure) is not only variable among Kirtland's Warbler WMA stands, but also within individual stands. In some areas regeneration methods have left a "patchwork" pattern where small gaps have purposely been left unplanted in an effort to provide foraging habitat for nesting birds or have resulted from failed regeneration efforts. In other stands, natural disturbances (such as wildfire) have left a patchy distribution of overstory and understory stems.

Finally, other stands may have wetland areas or different soil types that do not lend themselves to jack pine forest ecosystems. A good example of this pattern can be found in a stand located in Oscoda County. Using the on-screen digitizing tool in Arc-GIS® and 2005 1-m resolution NAIP orthophotography, we estimate that only 116 acres or 15 percent of the 780 acres total is considered Kirtland's Warbler habitat (between 5-23 years old). The remainder of the tract is dominated by wetlands in the interior (200 acres or 26 percent), older jack pine in the northwestern portion of the tract (200 acres or 26 percent), and mixed jack pine and hardwood in the eastern portion of the tract (265 acres or 33 percent). However, due to the heterogeneous nature of some stands, digital imagery should be examined or a site visit be made before making conclusions regarding the composition and structural characteristics of each stand.

Wildlife

Birds

The first known non-Kirtland's Warbler bird surveys conducted on the Kirtland's Warbler WMA occurred as part of the assessment work contracted by the Service in 2006 (Goebel et al. 2007). Sixty bird species were documented during point counts conducted in jack pine-dominated tracts; 75 percent were breeding species recorded on the evidence of singing males.

Whereas jack pine plantations provide food and shelter for a certain suite of species, other jack pine ecosystems offer habitat for a different suite of birds, many of which are either officially listed or of conservation priority (Table 2). Species that use mature jack stands include Black-backed Woodpecker, Spruce Grouse, and Olive-sided Flycatcher. In the younger jack pine stands and more open areas, many openland (grassland and shruland) birds of conservation concern breed. Species found in the early successional stages of jack pine ecosystems include (of course) Kirtland's Warbler, Palm Warbler, Black-billed Cuckoo, Brown Thrasher, Eastern Towhee, Prairie Warbler, and Nashville Warbler. The American Kestrel, Northern Harrier, Upland Sandpiper, and Clay-colored Sparrow can be found in the larger, more open areas.

Mammals

Based on state-wide distribution patterns (Kurta 2001), there are approximately 52 extant mammal species possible within the Kirtland's Warbler WMA (Appendix C). However, range expansion of some species is likely to occur soon. For instance, although not prevalent within the Lower Peninsula of Michigan now, gray wolf (a federally listed endangered species) is likely to become established in the future. Species of high public interest include river otter, beaver, snowshoe hare, and white-tailed deer.

Reptiles and Amphibians

Based on state-wide distribution patterns (multiple authors), 36 species of herptofauna possibly exist within the Kirtland's Warbler WMA and many of these species are of conservation priority (Appendix C). Much more inventory work is required at the Kirtland's Warbler WMA. Future considerations

Table 2: Bird Species Strongly Associated with Young, KW, and Old, Stands of the Kirtland's Warbler WMA

Young (Less than 5 years old)	KW (5-23 years old)	Old (More than 23 years old)
Indigo Bunting***	Kirtland's Warbler***	Eastern Wood-Pewee***
Eastern Bluebird***	Nashville Warbler***	Hermit Thrush***
Field Sparrow***	Eastern Towhee***	Ovenbird***
Lincoln's Sparrow***	Brown Thrasher**	Rose-breasted Grosbeak***
Black-billed Cuckoo*	Alder Flycatcher**	Red-breasted Nuthatch***
		Red-eyed Vireo***
		Black-capped Chickadee**
		Chipping Sparrow**
		Mourning Dove*

*P < 0.05; ** P < 0.01; *** P < 0.001.
Table 2 provides the results of a statistical procedure that assigns species to each of the three stand ages based on frequency of encounters. It also only shows species whose *P*-value is <0.05. Some species are also highly associated with these stands, but at greater *P*-values. See Figure 6 on page 27.

should be made to include management appropriate for other species of concern and rare species such as the Massasauga rattlesnake and Blanding's turtle.

Associated Plans and Initiatives

Michigan's Wildlife Action Plan

In 2005, Michigan's Wildlife Action Plan (WAP) was completed to better manage wildlife species and their habitats of "greatest conservation need" in Michigan. The plan was developed with the support of funding from the State Wildlife Grant Program created by Congress in 2001. The goal of the plan is to provide a common strategic framework that will enable Michigan's conservation partners to jointly implement a long-term holistic approach for the conservation of all wildlife species. Members of the partnership include the Michigan Department of Natural Resources, the U.S. Fish and Wildlife Service, the U.S. Forest Service, The Nature Conservancy, Michigan Natural Features Inventory, academics from several Michigan universities, as well as many other agencies and conservation organizations.

The action plan:

- provides an ecological , habitat-based framework to aid in the conservation and management of wildlife;

- identifies and recommends actions to improve habitat conditions and population status of species with the greatest conservation need (SGCN), which are those species with small or declining populations or other characteristics that make them vulnerable;

- recommends actions that will help to keep common species common;

- identifies and prioritizes conservation actions, research and survey needs, and long-term monitoring needed to assess the success of conservation efforts;

- complements other conservation strategies, funding sources, planning initiatives, and legally mandated activities;

- incorporates public participation to provide an opportunity for all conservation partners and Michigan residents to influence the future of resource management;

- provides guidance for use of State Wildlife Grant funds; and

- provides a clear process for review and revision as necessary to address changing conditions and to integrate new information as it becomes available.

Aerial photo of intensely managed jack pine plantations (left) and prescribed fire jack pine habitat (right).

Migratory Bird Conservation Initiatives

Several migratory bird conservation plans have been published over the last decade that can be used to help guide management decisions for the refuges and WMAs. Bird conservation planning efforts have evolved from a largely local, site-based orientation to a more regional, even inter-continental, landscape-oriented perspective. Several trans-national migratory bird conservation initiatives have emerged to help guide the planning and implementation process. The regional plans relevant to Kirtland's Warbler WMA are:

- The Upper M ississippi River/Gre at Lakes Joint Venture Implementation Plan of the North American Waterfowl Management Plan;

- The P artners in Flight Boreal Hardwood Transition [land] Bird Conservation Plan;

- The Upper Mississippi Valley/Great L akes Regional Shorebird Conservation Plan; and

- The Upper Mississippi Valley/Great L akes Regional Waterbird Conservation Plan.

All four conservation plans are integrated under the umbrella of the North American Bird Conservation Initiative. Each of the bird conservation initiatives has a process for designating priority species, modeled to a large extent on the Partners in Flight method of computing scores based on independent assessments of global relative abundance, breeding and wintering distribution, vulnerability to threats, area importance, and population trend. These scores are often used by agencies in developing lists of priority bird species. The Service based its 2001 list of Non-game Birds of Conservation Concern primarily on the Partners in Flight, shorebird, and waterbird status assessment scores.

Conservation Organization Plans

Several non-governmental organizations have implemented planning initiatives in the northern Lower Peninsula region. Plans and publications of note inclue *Michigan Important Bird Areas* (National Audubon Society, 2009), *Great Lakes Ecoregional Plan* (The Nature Conservancy, 2000) and the publication *Conservation Planning for the Grayling Subdistrict of Michigan* (Mulladore et al., 2006)

Nuisance Species Management

No inventories of invasive plants have been done at the Kirtland's Warbler WMA. However, it is known that some of the wetland areas contain pur - ple loosestrife (*Lythrum salicaria*) and that spotted knapweed (*Centaurea maculosa*) can be locally common in the openlands. Autumn olive (*Elae-agnus umbellata*) is not currently found in the jack pine systems, but does occur in richer soils nearby.

It is unknown what invasive species may come into jack pine ecosystem due to climate change. However, future planning will likely need to address such an issue and focus on early detection and rapid response efforts, and outreach to owners of nurseries or other potential vectors of invasive species and pathogens.

Control of the Brown-headed Cowbird is a vital part of Kirtland's Warbler management (Probst et al. 2003). Without Cowbird control, up to 70 percent of Kirtland's Warbler nests may be parasitized (Walkinshaw 1972). According to Chris Mensing (U.S. Fish & Wildlife Service, East Lasing Field Office), biologists from the East Lansing Field Office have trapped Brown-headed Cowbirds annually since 1972 in Kirtland's Warbler nesting areas to reduce nest parasitism. Traps are operated each year from mid-April through June, with trapping beginning approximately one month before Kirtland's Warblers arrive to take advantage of cowbird migration chronology and behavior. Cowbirds usually begin arriving in the northern Lower Peninsula of Michigan in April. At that time Cowbirds are in flocks and tend to exhibit a higher degree of social or gregarious behavior. This behavior seems to make them more susceptible to decoy trapping than later in the season when they disperse across the landscape to breed. Consequently, it is important to initiate trapping at approximately the time cowbirds arrive in the area for optimal trap effectiveness.

The decoy traps require live decoys for effective operation. The U.S. Department of Agriculture, Animal and Plant Health Inspection Service, Wildlife Services (USDA-APHIS-WS), at Sandusky, Ohio, capture and temporarily house the necessary cowbirds which arrive in northern Ohio each spring weeks before they arrive in northern Michigan.

In 2008, 3,135 Brown-headed Cowbirds were captured, 8.2 percent fewer birds than last year's total of 3,415. Since 1972, 140,040 cowbirds have been removed from Kirtland's Warbler nesting areas, averaging 3,893 per year. The 54 traps caught an average of 58 cowbirds per trap over 3,647 trap days. The number of cowbirds removed each year has increased 16 times and decreased 20 times during the 37 years of the program. This is likely due to normal fluctuations in the cowbird population, and may indicate that the trapping program has had no long-term effect on the area's Brown-headed Cowbird population.

Although a member of the native faunal community, the dramatic population increase noted in white-tailed deer numbers across much of the northern Lower Peninsula over the last century has resulted in numerous adverse effects to ecosystems, supporting the argument that the effects of over abundant deer may be as substantial as some exotic species. In some area of the Kirtland's Warbler WMA, deer densities are higher than desired. The effects of browsing may be locally intense, especially in the few hardwood stands found at the Kirtland's

Brown-headed Cowbirds are trapped to reduce Kirtland's Warbler nest parasitism. U.S. Fish & Wildlife Service photo.

Warbler WMA. Consideration should be given to liberalizing the take of this game species at the Kirtland's Warbler WMA.

Prescribed Fires

Prescribed fire is an effective way to regenerate jack pine stands and maintain younger stands for breeding warblers. In the past, prescribed and natural fires were the primary method of habitat creation used in the area. The first management action at Kirtland's Warbler WMA was a successful prescribed fire in 1992. However, the terrain and climate of the pine barrens, the history and threat of fire escape, and local residents' aversion to burning severely limit the use of fire for jack pine management.

Surveys and Censuses

Endangered and Threatened Species

Kirtland's Warbler WMA tracts are included as part of the annual Kirtland's Warbler census conducted by the Michigan Department of Natural Resources. It is estimated that, on average, 4 percent of the known world population of Kirtland's Warbler have been found on the WMA since 2000 (Table 3 on page 26). In occupied WMA stands, over three singing males have been recorded on average per sampling plot (Table 4 on page 26).

The first known non-Kirtland's Warbler wildlife surveys conducted on the Kirtland's Warbler WMA occurred as part of the assessment work contracted by the Service in 2006 (Goebel et al. 2007). Sixty bird species were documented during point counts conducted in jack pine-dominated tracts; 75 percent were breeding species recorded on the evidence of singing males. Bird communities and individual species abundance and frequency of encounter patterns generally differed among stand age classes (see Figure 6 on page 27 and Figure 7 on page 28).

Studies and Investigations

Research is an integral component of land management for wildlife population preservation, conservation, and restoration and should be incorporated along with future inventory and monitoring. Historically, the majority of research on many refuges pertained to single species of wildlife and their habitats. However, as theories and concepts regarding wildlife and habitat management have changed, so too should the focus of research. For instance, in recent years, upland research in the

Table 3: Number of Kirtland's Warbler Singing Males by Year (2000-2005) at Kirtland's Warbler Wildlife Management Area

Year	Number of Singing Males	Percentage (%) of Total Michigan Singing Male Population
2000	5	0.6
2001	30	2.8
2002	27	2.6
2003	59	4.9
2004	72	5.3
2005	100	7.0
2006	124	8.4
2007	137	8.1
Average (±1SD)	48.8 (34.7)	3.9 (2.3)
Data provided by K. Kintigh (MDNR)		

Table 4: Parcel-level Abundance Values for Kirtland's Warbler Singing Males Recorded at Kirtland's Warbler WMA

Stand Age Class	County	Tract-ID	Sampling Points	Singing KW per sampling point
KW	Clare	CL-08	2	3.00
KW	Clare	CL-11	1	3.00
KW	Clare	CL-18	3	4.33
KW	Clare	CL-21	2	5.00
KW	Crawford	CR-09	1	4.00
KW	Crawford	CR-10	1	3.00
KW	Oscoda	OS-02	6	2.50
KW	Oscoda	OS-03	2	3.50
KW	Oscoda	OS-14	1	2.00
KW	Oscoda	OS-18	1	1.00
KW	Ogemaw	OG-26	3	4.33
KW	Ogemaw	OG-28	4	1.75
YOUNG	Ogemaw	OG-01	1	1.00
YOUNG	Ogemaw	OG-25	1	4.00
		TOTAL	29	3.07

Figure 6: Number of Singing Kirtland's Warbler Males Per Sample Point, Kirtland's Warbler WMA

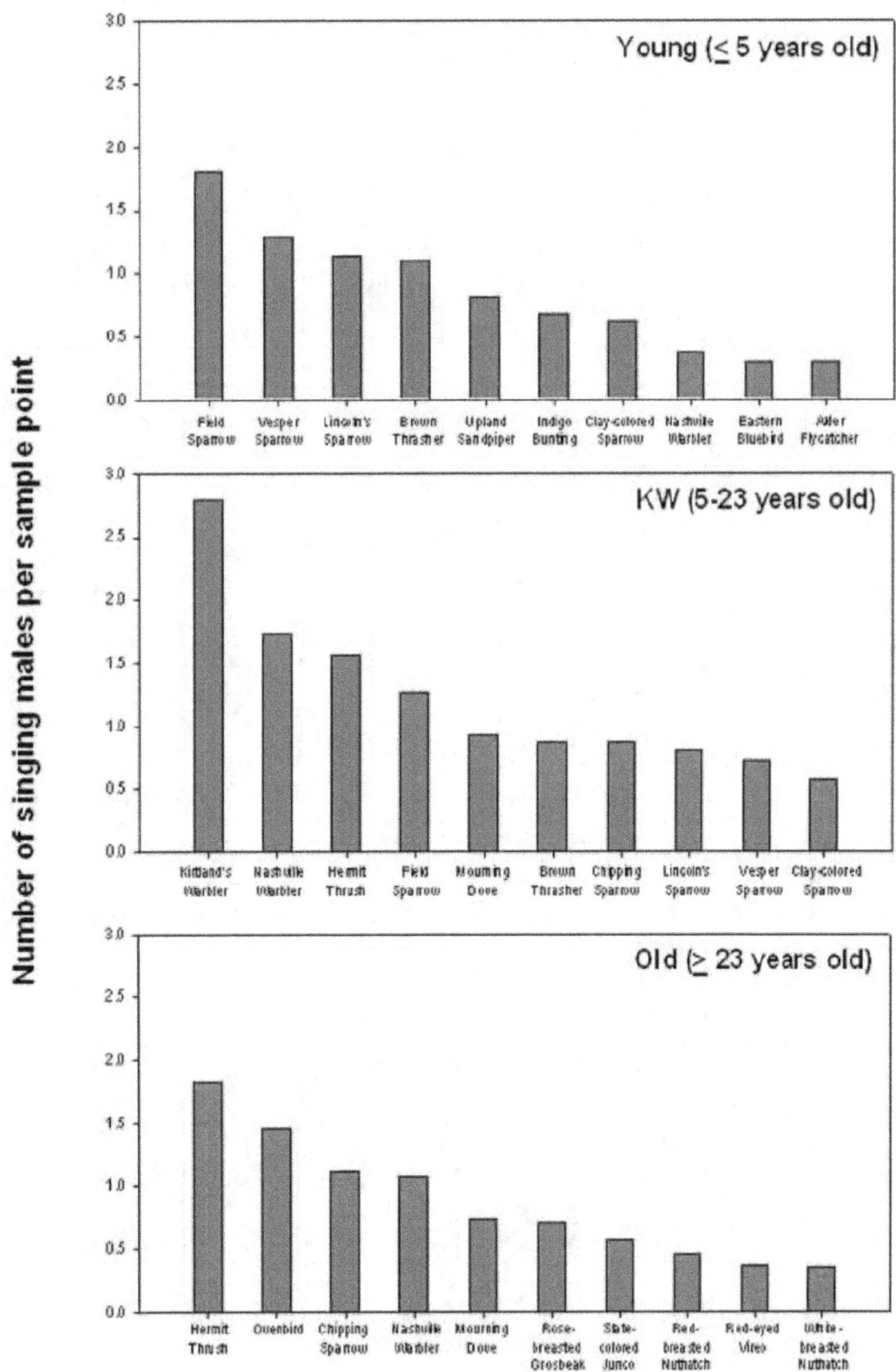

Figure 7: Frequency of Bird Occurrence Within Sample Stands, Kirtland's Warbler WMA

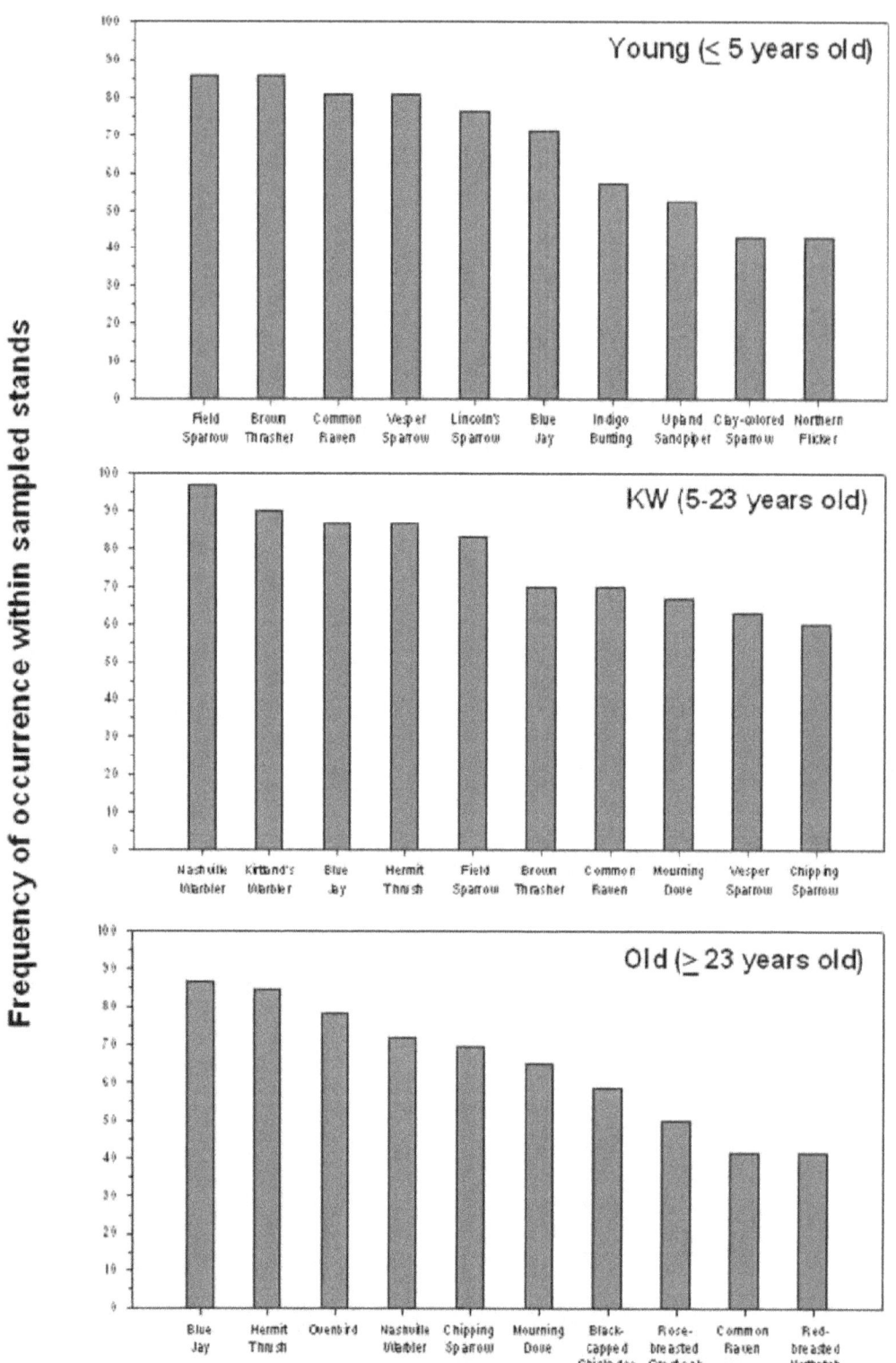

region has increasingly been focused on ecosystem patterns and processes, such as the ecological disturbance history of forest stands in the context of restoration of stand composition and structure in stands altered by past human activities. Future research should continue to pursue aspects of disturbance ecology, restoration ecology, landscape ecology, forest ecology, and conservation biology and related fields in the context of wildlife habitat conservation, preservation, and restoration at the Kirtland's Warbler WMA. Other future research should examine the effects of invasive species and climate change on ecosystem patterns and processes.

Coordination Activities

The Seney NWR staff who manage Kirtland's Warbler WMA invest a significant amount of energy and time representing the WMA in its role as a partner with other resource agencies and non-government organizations. The Refuge Manager serves as a member of the Kirtland's Warber Recovery Team and the Refuge Forester participates as a team member on various committees and groups.

Visitor Services

The 1997 National Wildlife Refuge System Improvement Act emphasizes wildlife management and that all prospective public uses on any given unit of the Refuge System must be found to be compatible with the wildlife-related purposes before they can be allowed. The Refuge System Improvement Act also identifies six priority uses of national wildlife refuges that in most cases will be considered compatible uses:

- wildlife observation
- wildlife photography
- hunting
- fishing
- environmental education
- interpretation of nature

Opportunities to participate in all of these wildlife-dependent activities, with the exception of fishing, exist at Kirtland's Warbler WMA.

Hunting

Kirtland's Warbler WMA is open for hunting of all legal game species in Michigan per state regulations. However, little is known regarding the statistics regarding hunting use. Due to the nature of the habitats at the Management Area, the species most

Black bear. U.S. Fish & Wildlife Service photo

likely hunted are white-tailed deer, Wild Turkey, Ruffed Grouse, snowshoe hare, American Woodcock, and black bear. In early successional stands (recent clear cuts waiting regeneration for Kirtland's Warbler) hunting is probably limited to Wild Turkey and white-tailed deer. As stands mature and become close-canopy with more mature trees, more species are hunted and more hunting likely occurs. The use of bait, snowmobiles, or ATVs is prohibited.

Fishing

Although a few parcels of the Management Area are adjacent to streams, most parcels do not have fishable waters. Fishing is likely not a very common event at Kirtland's Warbler WMA.

Photography, Wildlife Observation, Environmental Education and Interpretation

The majority of the Visitor Services that are provided by the Kirtland's Warbler WMA are interwoven into the yearly Kirtland's Warbler tours conducted by the Service's East Lansing Field Office, Michigan Audubon Society and the U. S. Forest Service. According to Service records, during 2008 a total of 775 people from 40 states and three foreign countries attended a tour to see Kirtland's Warbler and hear about habitat management. These tours occur yearly from May 15 to July 4.

Although parcels inhabited by Kirtland's Warbler during the breeding season are closed to entry, uninhabited areas and the network of two-track roads that connect them afford photographers of all skill levels opportunities to photograph wildlife and excellent hiking and biking opportunities.

Archaeological and Cultural Resources Management

No active cultural resources management occurs on the Kirtland's Warbler WMA. In general, cultural resources management in the Service is the responsibility of the Regional Director and is not delegated to field managers for the Section 106 process when historic properties could be affected by Service undertakings, for issuing archeological permits, and for Indian tribal involvement. The Regional Historic Preservation Officer advises the Regional Director about procedures, compliance, and implementation of cultural resources laws. The field manager assists by informing the Regional Historic Preservation Officer about Service undertakings, by protecting archeological sites and historic properties, by monitoring archeological investigations by contractors and permittees, and by reporting violations.

Law Enforcement

Kirtland's Warbler WMA is dedicated to safeguarding the resources under its jurisdiction, including natural resources, cultural resources, and facilities. Resource management on the WMA includes both protective and preventive functions. Protection is safeguarding the visiting public, staff, facilities and natural and cultural resources from criminal action, accidents, negligence and acts of nature such as wildfires. Preventing incidents from occurring is the best form of protection and requires a known and visible law enforcement presence as well as other proactive steps to address potential threats and natural hazards.

Over the years, the most common violations on the Kirtland's Warbler WMA have been vandalism and trespass. Vandalism incidents have included damage to signs and other structures and dumping on side roads.

Chapter 4: Future Management Direction: Tomorrow's Vision

Goals, Objectives and Strategies

The planning team developed goals and objectives for three management alternatives at Kirtland's Warbler WMA. Cooperating agencies, conservation organizations and Seney NWR staff all participated in this endeavor. The three alternatives were:

- Alternative 1: Current Direction of Habitat Management (No Action)

- Alternative 2: Management from an Ecological Perspective

- Alternative 3: Ecological Management and Land Ownership Consolidation (Preferred Alternative)

The preferred alternative, Ecological Management and Land Ownership Consolidation forms the basis for the Kirtland's Warbler WMA CCP and the goals, objectives and strategies presented on the following pages. The planning team established goals for the WMA as a whole, objectives for achieving those goals, and the specific strategies that will be employed by Refuge staff. The goals are organized into the broad categories of wildlife, habitat, and people.

Three goals were established for Kirtland's Warbler WMA:

- Goal 1: Wildlife – Management will play an integral role in the recovery of the Kirtland's Warbler. Kirtland's Warbler WMA lands will support the broad array of wildlife species that are dependent on each seral stage of the jack pine ecosystems (from barrens to mature jack pine).

Spruce Grouse. U.S. Fish & Wildlife Service photo.

- Goal 2: Habitat – Manage habitat to support Kirtland's Warblers and associated wildlife species by providing near benchmark conditions across all seral stages of the jack pine ecosystem. Employ sound management practices that emulate patterns of structure and composition resulting from wildfire and other natural disturbances.

- Goal 3: People – Encourage the public to explore jack pine ecosystems and learn about its associated wildlife.

Goal 1: Wildlife

Management will play an integral role in the recovery of the Kirtland's Warbler. Kirtland's Warbler WMA lands will support the broad array of wildlife species that are dependent on each seral stage of the jack pine ecosystems (from barrens to mature jack pine).

Objective 1.1

Continue to be an active partner in the Kirtland's Warbler recovery effort.

American badger. U.S. Fish & Wildlife Service photo

Rationale: The Kirtland's Warbler WMA was established in 1980, under authority of the Endangered Species Act, to aid in the recovery of the Kirtland's Warbler. Since that time, the Service has been an active participant in a partnership that has brought the Kirtland's Warbler population from the brink of extinction to numbers surpassing the recovery objective for the last 7 years. Guided by the Kirtland's Warbler Recovery Team, this partnership has developed techniques to census the population, limit nest parasitism, and regenerate jack pine to create suitable nesting habitat.

Examples of Service Resource Conservation Priority Species that will benefit under this management include: Black-billed Cuckoo, Field Sparrow, Northern Flicker, and Upland Sandpiper.

Strategies:

1. Participate in the annual Kirtland's Warbler Census to aid in monitoring the population trends.

2. Work with Ecological Services to continue annual trapping efforts to remove Brown-headed Cowbirds from nesting areas and explore new ways to eliminate Cowbirds parasitism of Kirtland's Warbler nests.

3. Coordinate harvest and regeneration of jack pine on Kirtland's Warbler WMA lands with the Michigan DNR to ensure that the Services lands are contributing to the Kirtland's Warbler recovery effort.

4. Conduct and participate in research to better understand the ecology and management of Kirtland's Warbler populations.

Objective 1.2

By 2016, implement a monitoring program to track the presence, abundance, population trends, and/or habitat associations of Trust Resources and determine ways to emulate natural species diversity.

Rationale: The jack pine ecosystem is known to support a vast array of wildlife, many of which are listed as Resource Conservation Priority Species in Region 3 of the U.S. Fish & Wildlife Service. Since the creation of the Kirtland's Warbler WMA, recovery of Kirtland's Warbler has been the only goal of its management. Now, with Kirtland's Warbler populations exceeding recovery goals for 7 consecutive years, the Service has an opportunity to manage more from an ecological perspective and benefit species across the seral stages of the jack pine ecosystem. Research should be conducted to determine how to best manage the Kirtland's Warbler WMA for all Trust Species, without diminishing its contribution to Kirtland's Warbler recovery.

Strategies:

1. Determine the presence, abundance and habitat associations of Trust Resources currently using Kirtland's Warbler WMA lands.

2. Develop and implement a monitoring program to track population trends, and/or habitat associations of Trust Resources.

3. Conduct annual reviews of trends to determine if there are priorities for research or management.

4. If a Trust Resource research or management issue is identified, initiate action at the local level. If the issue goes beyond the boundary of the Kirtland's Warbler WMA, take the lead role in coordinating with federal, state, and non-government organization partners to develop broader scale projects to resolve issues.

Goal 2: Habitat

Manage habitat to support Kirtland's Warblers and associated wildlife species by providing near benchmark conditions across all seral stages of the jack pine ecosystem. Employ sound management practices that emulate patterns of structure and composition resulting from wildfire and other natural disturbances.

Objective 2.1

Continue to manage jack pine stands in conjunction with the Michigan DNR, but place greater emphasis on promoting ecological integrity within managed stands.

Rationale: Michigan DNR forest managers have devised a system of intensively managing jack pine that provide suitable nesting habitat for the Kirtland's Warbler. However these plantations are ecologically simplified and lack the diversity of stands produced by the natural disturbance mechanism, wildfire. This loss of structural and compositional diversity has negatively impacted populations of many wildlife species in Michigan.

Future management should consider all seral stages of jack pine ecosystem development, from barrens to mature forest, and strive to emulate natural conditions in each stage. This is important, because each stage offers habitat for a different suite of species, many of which are on the U.S. Fish and Wildlife Service Conservation Priority list. Young stands (grassland and shrubland) can provide breeding habitat for openland birds, including Upland Sandpiper, Prairie Warbler, and Clay-colored Sparrow. Bird species that use later seral stages or the "biological legacies" of these stands include Red Crossbill, Black-backed Woodpecker and Olive-sided Flycatcher.

Strategies:

1. Work with federal, state and local officials to garner support for the use of prescribed fire in the management of jack pine to create Kirtland's Warbler nesting habitat.

2. Work with federal, state and local fire officials to employ prescribed fire as a management tool where it can be applied safely without risk to life and property.

3. Elsewhere, attempt to emulate the compositional and structural patterns of jack pine stands resulting from wildfire through

mechanical treatments (i.e. timber sales). Place increased emphasis on maintaining "legacy" trees (e.g., large red and white pine, red and white oak, etc.) and providing more (and larger) standing snags and coarse woody debris.

4. Parcels that contain habitats other than jack pine will be managed to emulate patterns resulting from natural disturbances.

5. Develop research demonstration sites that exemplify ecologically-based jack pine management and illustrate how emulating natural conditions can provide multiple species benefits.

6. Develop a map and monitor spotted knapweed distribution within and near Kirtland's Warbler WMA parcels. Initiate removal if the species spreads into nesting areas.

Objective 2.2

Within 5 years of completion of this CCP, develop a land consolidation plan for the Kirtland's Warbler WMA that maintains or increases habitat for the warbler and increases management efficiency for all agencies involved.

Rationale: The Kirtland's Warbler WMA consists of 125 separate tracts of land located in eight counties of Michigan's northern Lower Peninsula. Their size ranges from 2 to 600 acres and most tracts are located within larger tracts of land owned by the state of Michigan. There is no local office or dedi-

Mechanical treatment of mature jack pine to prepare site for replanting of jack pine for Kirtland's Warbler, Kirtland's Warbler WMA.

cated staff assigned to the Kirtland's Warbler WMA; staff at the Seney NWR, which is located between 150 and 300 miles from most parcels, is responsible for administrative oversight. Currently, management is accomplished through a cooperative agreement between the Service and the Michigan DNR. Under this agreement, the Service retains ownership and oversight functions on Kirtland's Warbler WMA lands while the Michigan DNR determines when timber on a given parcel should be cut and regenerated. The Service is responsible for the timber harvest and the DNR contracts for replanting services.

Consolidation of Kirtland's Warbler WMA lands is being considered to increase management efficiency. Currently the travel distances between Seney NWR and WMA lands limits administrative oversight and management effectiveness. Due to their small size, WMA lands cannot be managed independent of the surrounding landscape. Therefore a high degree of coordination with the Michigan DNR is required to accomplish any meaningful management.

A consolidation has the potential to increase the amount of land dedicated to Kirtland's Warbler management. Both state and federal regulations require that lands exchanged be equal, based on an appraisal value, not acreage. Consequently, if the state were to exchange lands not currently managed for the Kirtland's Warbler for Service land with a higher appraised value, there would be a net gain because the Service would manage its new lands for the warbler. This scenario is likely because of the variation in land values from county to county.

The Service has completed many land exchanges with states, including six with the state of Michigan in the last 20 years. The primary purpose of most of these exchanges was to improve management efficiency. The Service will always have the option to retain the Kirtland's Warbler WMA name for any new lands acquired. Thus, if consolidation is achieved, we would effectively be moving the Kirtland's Warbler WMA to a new location. The most significant benefit of consolidation would be increasing habitat to further ensure full recovery and long-term survival the species. In addition, consolidation would result in larger parcels owned and managed under each agency. Larger parcels allow for improved control and prevention of invasive species and reduced habitat fragmentation.

The concept of land consolidation is supported by all agencies involved in Kirtland's Warbler management. In general, the Service, the Michigan DNR, and the U.S. Forest Service would seek lands to exchange amongst the agencies to consolidate ownership and increase the land base managed for the Kirtland's Warbler habitat. Public input on any exchange proposal would be sought in compliance with the National Environmental Policy Act. All parties recognize that any exchanges may take years to complete, but they agree it will be worth the effort.

Background:

The idea of consolidating lands has been discussed since inception of the Kirtland's Warbler WMA more that 25 years ago. In a letter dated November 13, 1979, from Wayne H. Tody, Deputy Director of the Bureau of Resources for the Michigan DNR to Harvey K. Nelson, Regional Director for Region 3 of the Service, land consolidation is listed as a condition for support of a federal Kirtland's Warbler land acquisition program in Michigan. The 1991 cooperative agreement between the Service and Michigan DNR states that they mutually agree "to exchange interest in land of high nesting habitat capability where necessary for effective management." In addition, we understand that the Michigan DNR is working to implement a Land Consolidation Strategy. We believe that the CCP planning process and the Land Consolidation Strategy make the timing right to fully explore land consolidation.

On February 21, 2007, members of the Kirtland's Warbler Recovery Team met at the Michigan DNR, Gaylord Operations Center, at the Service's request to discuss the CCP and alternatives for future management of the Kirtland's Warbler WMA. Nearly all members of the team attended as well as additional staff from local DNR offices, several Service field stations, and representatives from the U.S. Forest Service and two universities. The primary purpose of this meeting was to explore the possibility of consolidating the widespread land holdings of the Kirtland's Warbler WMA for more efficient management by all agencies that manage land for Kirtland's Warbler habitat.

It was decided at the February meeting that a smaller interagency committee should convene to formulate specific land consolidation proposals. The members of this committee should be land manag-

Table 5: Sites Identified for Potential Exchange

Location	Concept	Potential Sites
Northern Lower Peninsula	Large acreage of Service lands currently exists. Exchanges would include Michigan DNR and Service lands only and would create fewer and larger parcels.	■ Pere Cheney Management Area - Staley Lake Mgmt. Area, ■ NW Ogemaw Management Area, ■ Leota Management Area, ■ Big Creek Management Area
Northern Lower Peninsula	Create fewer and larger parcels closer to Seney NWR, but still within the northern lower Peninsula. Exchanges would include only Michigan DNR and Service lands.	■ Clear Lake
Northern Lower Peninsula	Consolidate into fewer, larger parcels and include Service, Forest Service and Michigan DNR lands.	■ Wurtsmith Block to Forest Service, Michigan DNR gets all Service lands, and Service gets unidentified Forest Service lands (multiple compartments).
Upper Peninsula	Maintain close proximity to Seney NWR; opportunity to use prescribed fire as a management tool; minimal impact to existing ORV trails. Consolidation will only involve Service and Michigan DNR lands.	■ M-94 southwest of Seney NWR, ■ M-28 lands north of Seney NWR, ■ Danaher Plains Complex, ■ Ishpeming Area, ■ Big Two-Hearted River Country, ■ Private lands purchased in the Upper Peninsula by Michigan DNR going to the Service, Michigan DNR getting northern Lower Peninsula Service lands, ■ Baraga Plains, ■ Yellow Dog Plains.

ers or biologists with specific knowledge of affected lands and Kirtland's Warbler management. The preliminary proposals will then be presented to each agency's leadership for review and recommendation.

The interagency committee met on April 10, 2008 in Grayling, Michigan. Attendees included three representatives from Michigan DNR, two from the U.S. Forest Service and three from the U.S. Fish and Wildlife Service. The committee concluded this meeting with a list of ideas for future land consolidation. These ideas are presented in the following paragraphs as a set of guidelines. These guidelines may be refined as individual agency discussions move forward and specific planning continues in the next several years.

Land Consolidation Guidelines:

1. Lands must be manageable for Kirtland's Warbler (i.e. sites of sufficient size with jack pine as a major constituent of seral stages).

2. Must improve management efficiency for all agencies involved.

3. No substantial buildings or improvements.

4. Sites do not contain hazardous materials or environmental contaminants.

Sites Identified for Possible Exchange:

The sites described in Table 5 were suggested by the interagency committee that met in April 2008 as possibilities to explore for an exchange. These sites are mentioned for illustration purposes only; no official endorsement has been sought or obtained through the U.S. Fish and Wildlife Service, the Michigan DNR or U.S. Forest Service.

Strategies:

1. Interagency team will follow land consolidation guidelines to establish priority exchange scenarios.

2. Land apprai sals, following federal and st ate guidelines, will be conducted on all lands identified for exchange.

Goal 3: People

Encourage the public to explore jack pine ecosystems and learn about its associated wildlife.

Objective 3.1: Hunting

Provide the public with opportunities to hunt on Kirtland's Warbler WMA lands in accordance with state and federal regulations.

Rationale: Kirtland's Warbler WMA is open for hunting of all legal game species in Michigan per state regulations. However, little is known regarding the statistics regarding hunting use. Due to the nature of the habitats at the Management Area, most hunting is likely confined to white-tailed deer, Wild Turkey, Ruffed Grouse, snowshoe hare, American Woodcock, and black bear. In early successional stands (recent clear cuts waiting regeneration for Kirtland's Warbler) hunting is probably confined to Wild Turkey and white-tailed deer. As stands mature and become close-canopy with more mature trees, more species are hunted and more hunting likely occurs. The use of bait, snowmobiles, or ATVs are prohibited on Service lands.

Strategies:

1. Increase law enforcem ent on Ser vice properties to ensure consistency with federal hunting regulations (e.g. no deer baiting, permanent blinds, bear hunting with dogs, and off-road vehicle use).

2. In coope ration with the Michigan DNR, pro - duce maps to show the hunting public areas subject to federal regulations.

Objective 3.2: Wildlife Observation, Wildlife Photography, Environmental Education and Environmental Interpretation

Within 5 years of approval of the plan, increase opportunities for wildlife observation and photography, environmental education and interpreta-

Interpretive sign at Kirtland's Warbler WMA. U.S. Fish & Wildlife Service photo.

tion to correspond with an increase (from 2008 level) in WMA visitation. The level of knowledge about, and the positive attitude toward, the WMA will increase among visitors throughout the next 15 years.

Rationale: The majority of the visitor services that are provided by the Kirtland's Warbler WMA are interwoven into the yearly Kirtland's Warbler tours conducted by the U.S. Fish and Wildlife Service's East Lansing Field Office, Michigan Audubon Society, and the U. S. Forest Service. According to Service records, during 2008 a total of 775 people from 40 states and three foreign countries attended a tour to see Kirtland's Warbler and hear about habitat management. These tours occur yearly from May 15 to July 4.

Although parcels inhabited by Kirtland's Warbler during the breeding season are closed to entry, uninhabited areas and the network of two-track roads that connect them afford photographers of all skill levels opportunities to photograph wildlife and hiking and biking activities.

Strategies:

1. Continue ac tive support of the annual Kirt - land's Warbler Festival and Tours.

2. Encourage wildlife-dependent activities o n Kirtland's Warbler WMA lands by providing outreach materials, such as brochures and displays, at local public events and in community facilities.

Chapter 5: Plan Implementation

New and Existing Projects

This CCP outlines an ambitious course of action for the future management of the Kirtland's Warbler WMA. The ability to enhance wildlife habitats on the Area and provide additional quality public use opportunities will require a significant commitment of staff and funding from the Service. The WMA will continually need appropriate operational and maintenance funding to implement the objectives in this plan.

The following provides a brief description of the highest priority projects for Kirtland's Warbler WMA, as chosen by the Seney NWR staff and listed in the Refuge Operating Needs System (RONS). Staffing, maintenance and operation needs will change if land consolidation occurs in the future.

Kirtland's Warbler WMA Operating Needs Projects

Enhance Refuge Management and Administration

- Hire an onsight resource specialist to coordinate management efforts, interface with the public and provide oversight of WMA lands. Estimated cost: $150,000

- Hire a technician to conduct wildlife surveys, post boundaries and oversee timber harvest and habitat regeneration. Estimated cost: $120,000

- Post boundaries of the WMA. Currently no boundaries are posted. Surveys need to be conducted and posts and signs purchased. A contract to post the boundary, in accordance with the Refuge Mannual, would be awarded. Estimated cost: $200,000

- Provide for public use by designating trails, constructing observation blinds and developing interpretive signs. Estimated cost: $100,000

A contractor plants trees at Kirtland's Warbler WMA. U.S. Fish & Wildlife Service photo.

- Habitat regeneration is a critical component of managing Kirtland's Warbler populations. Given the current size of the WMA, 300 acres would need to be regenerated annually at a minimum cost of $100 per acre. Estimated cost: $30,000

- Law enforcement is a necessary component of land management at the Kirtland's Warbler WMA. Funds are needed to hire a full-time law enforcement officer to ensure the protection of nesting areas during the breeding season, that hunting regulations are followed and that habitat is not destroyed by illegal timber harvest, off-road vehicles or other means. Estimated cost: $150,000

- Fire management is necessary to protect and manage habitat. A Fire Management Officer would be hired to coordinate fire suppression and prescribed burning with State and Service officials. Estimated cost: $200,000

- Establish an office and hire administrative support. To fully manage the Kirtland's Warbler WMA an office would need to be established to house the Resource Specialist and Technician. This office would need an Office Automation Clerk to manage the office and serve as a contact point for the public. Estimated cost: $100,000

Current and Future Staffing Requirements

The Kirtland's Warbler WMA does not have a permanent staff. The staff at Seney NWR oversees the WMA and provides limited services on an as-needed basis. These duties include, but are not limited to, administration of timber sales, coordinating with the state on harvesting and replanting efforts, participation in Kirtland's Warbler Recovery Team efforts, research, the Kirtland's Warber census, Cowbird trapping, public education and on-site law enforcement. Full-time oversight may be required in the future if the land holdings of the Kirtland's Warbler WMA are consolidated.

Step-down Management Plans

Step-down management plans describe specific actions that support the accomplishment of objectives. The Kirtland's Warbler WMA does not require many step-down plans due to relatively small size of properties, limited activities and the lack of staff and funding. The objectives and strategies outlined in this CCP will provide adequate detail for most of the programs at the Kirtland's Warbler WMA.

Partnership Opportunities

Partnerships have become an essential element for the successful accomplishments of Kirtland's Warbler WMA goals, objectives, and strategies. The objectives outlined in this CCP need the support and the partnerships of federal, state and local agencies, non-governmental organizations and individual citizens. This broad-based approach to man-

Baiting a Brown-headed Cowbird trap at Kirtland's Warbler WMA. U.S. Fish & Wildlife Service photo.

aging fish and wildlife resources extends beyond social and political boundaries and requires a broad foundation of support. The Kirtland's Warbler WMA will continue to seek creative partnership opportunities to achieve its vision for the future.

Notable existing partners include:

- Michigan DNR
- East Lansing Field Office, U.S. Fish and Wildlife Service
- U.S. Forest Service
- Kirtland Community College
- Michigan Audubon Society
- The Nature Conservancy

Wilderness Review

As part of the CCP process, we reviewed lands within the legislative boundaries of Kirtland's Warbler WMA for wilderness suitability. No lands were found suitable for designation as Wilderness as defined in the Wilderness Act of 1964. The WMA does not contain 5,000 contiguous, roadless acres nor does it have any units of sufficient size to make their preservation practicable as Wilderness. Lands acquired for the Kirtland's Warbler WMA have been substantially affected by humans, particularly through intense forestry, agriculture and transportation infrastructure.

Monitoring and Evaluation

The direction set forth in this CCP and specifically identified strategies and projects will be monitored throughout the life of this plan. On a periodic basis, the Regional Office will assemble a station review team whose purpose will be to visit the Kirtland's Warbler WMA and evaluate current activities in light of this plan. The team will review all aspects of management, including direction, accomplishments and funding. The goals and objectives presented in this CCP will provide the baseline from which this field station will be evaluated.

Climate Change Evaluation

The potential impacts of climate change will receive increasing attention and study during the life of this plan. All strategies for plan implementation, including consolidation of land holdings of the Kirtland's Warbler WMA, will be periodically evaluated in the light of new predictions and progress in carbon emission reduction.

Plan Review and Revision

The CCP for Kirtland's Warbler WMA is meant to provide guidance to managers and staff over the next 15 years. However, the CCP is also a dynamic and flexible document and several of the strategies contained in this plan are subject to such things as drought, floods, windstorms and other uncontrollable events. Likewise, many of the strategies are dependent upon Service funding for staff and projects. Because of all these factors, the recommendations in the CCP will be reviewed periodically and, if necessary, revised to meet new circumstances.

Appendix A: Environmental Assessment

Kirtland's Warbler

Wildlife Management Area

Environmental Assessment

Finding of No Significant Impact

Environmental Assessment and Comprehensive Conservation Plan for the Kirtland's Warbler Wildlife Management Area, Michigan

An Environmental Assessment (EA) has been prepared to identify management strategies to meet the conservation goals of the Kirtland's Warbler Wildlife Management Area. The EA examined the environmental consequences that each management alternative could have on the quality of the physical, biological, and human environment, as required by the National Environmental Policy Act of 1969 (NEPA). The EA evaluated three alternatives for the future management of Kirtland's Warbler WMA.

The alternative selected for implementation on the refuge is *Alternative 3*. The preferred alternative for Kirtland's Warbler WMA over the next 15 years directs management towards a more ecologically broad and holistic jack pine ecosystem management standpoint based on benchmark conditions derived from jack pine stands regenerated by wildfire. This alternative would include management practices that place a greater emphasis on ecological integrity and better emulating wildfire-produced jack pine stand composition and structural patterns and resulting biodiversity. An increased emphasis would also occur within law enforcement and visitor use. Land exchanges with the State, and possibly the U.S. Forest Service, to consolidate State and WMA parcels would be explored. Proposed land exchanges would likely increase the total area of land managed for Kirtland's Warbler, as well as increase management efficiency by both Federal and State agencies.

For reasons presented above and below, and based on an evaluation of the information contained in the Environmental Assessment, we have determined that the action of adopting Alternative 3 as the management alternative for Kirtland's Warbler WMA is not a major federal action which would significantly affect the quality of the human environment, within the meaning of Section 102 (2)(c) of the National Environmental Policy Act of 1969.

Additional Reasons:

1. Future management actions will have a neutral or positive impact on the local economy.
2. This action will not have an adverse impact on threatened or endangered species.

Supporting References:

Environmental Assessment
Comprehensive Conservation Plan

_____   9/10/09
Regional Director   Date

ACTING

ENVIRONMENTAL ASSESSMENT FOR IMPLEMENTATION OF COMPREHENSIVE CONSERVATION PLAN FOR KIRTLAND'S WARBLER WILDLIFE MANAGEMENT AREA

Abstract: The U.S. Fish and Wildlife Service is proposing to implement a Comprehensive Conservation Plan (CCP) for Kirtland's Warbler Wildlife Management Area (WMA) located in the northern Lower Peninsula of Michigan. This Environmental Assessment considers the biological, environmental and socioeconomic effects that implementing the CCP (which is the preferred alternative in this assessment), or an alternative, would have on the issues and concerns identified during the planning process. The purpose of the proposed action is to establish the management direction for the WMA for the next 15 years. The management action will be achieved by implementing a detailed set of goals, objectives, and strategies described in the CCP.

Responsible Agency and Official:

Thomas O. Melius, Regional Director
U.S. Fish & Wildlife Service
Bishop Henry Whipple Building
1 Federal Drive
Ft. Snelling, MN 55111

Contacts for additional information about this project:

Tracy Casselman, Manager

Kirtland's Warbler Wildlife Management Area
1674 Refuge Entrance Road
Seney, MI 49883
Office Phone: (906) 586-9851
Fax: (906) 586-3800

Gary Muehlenhardt

U.S. Fish & Wildlife Service
NWRS/Conservation Planning
Bishop Henry Whipple Building
1 Federal Drive
Ft. Snelling, MN 55111

Chapter 1: Purpose and Need

1.1. Background

The purpose of the proposed action is to specify a management direction for the Kirtland's Warbler Wildlife Management Area (WMA) for the next 15 years. This management direction will be described in detail through a set of goals, objectives, and strategies in a Comprehensive Conservation Plan (CCP).

Kirtland's Warbler WMA was established in 1980 in response to the need for more land dedicated to the recovery of this species. The U.S. Fish and Wildlife Service established Kirtland's Warbler WMA, in part, based upon the recommendations of the Kirtland's Warbler Recovery Team. The original goal was to acquire 7,500 acres of land on which habitat would be managed for the benefit of Kirtland's Warbler. At present, the area contains 125 separate tracts totaling 6,684 acres. While management for Kirtland's Warbler is paramount, the WMA provides habitat for a diversity of wildlife species (including a number of Regional Priority Species), both migratory and non-migratory.

We prepared this Environmental Assessment (EA) using guidelines established under the National Environmental Policy Act (NEPA) of 1969. NEPA requires us to examine the effects of proposed actions on the natural and human environment. In the following sections we describe three alternatives for future management of WMA lands, the environmental consequences of each alternative, and our preferred management direction. We have selected our preferred alternative based on environmental consequences and the ability to achieve the WMA's purpose.

1.2. Purpose

The purpose of the proposed action is to specify management directions for Kirtland's Warbler WMA over the coming 15 years. These management directions will be described in detail through a distinct set of goals, objectives, and strategies in a CCP.

The action is needed because adequate, long-term management direction does not currently exist for the Kirtland's Warbler WMA. Management is now guided by various general policies and short-term plans. The action is also needed to address current management issues and to satisfy the legislative mandates of the National Wildlife Refuge System Improvement Act of 1997, which requires the preparation of a CCP for all national wildlife refuge system lands in the United States.

1.3. Need for Action

The CCP ultimately derived from this EA will establish the overall management direction for the Kirtland's Warbler WMA over the next 15 years. The WMA currently lacks a long-term management plan. Instead, management is broadly guided at present by general Service policies, by interpreting the official purposes for which the Kirtland's Warbler WMA was created, and by short-term, step-down management plans.

The action is needed to address current management issues and to satisfy the legislative mandates of the National Wildlife Refuge System Improvement Act of 1997, which requires the preparation of a CCP for all national wildlife refuge lands in the United States.

This EA will present three management alternatives for the future of Kirtland's Warbler WMA. The preferred alternative will be selected based on its ability to meet identified goals. These goals may also be considered as the primary need for action. Goals for the WMA were developed by the planning team and encompass all aspects of management, including wildlife management, habitat management, and public use. Each of the management alternatives described in this EA will be able to at least minimally achieve these goals.

Figure 1: Kirtland's Warbler WMA Location

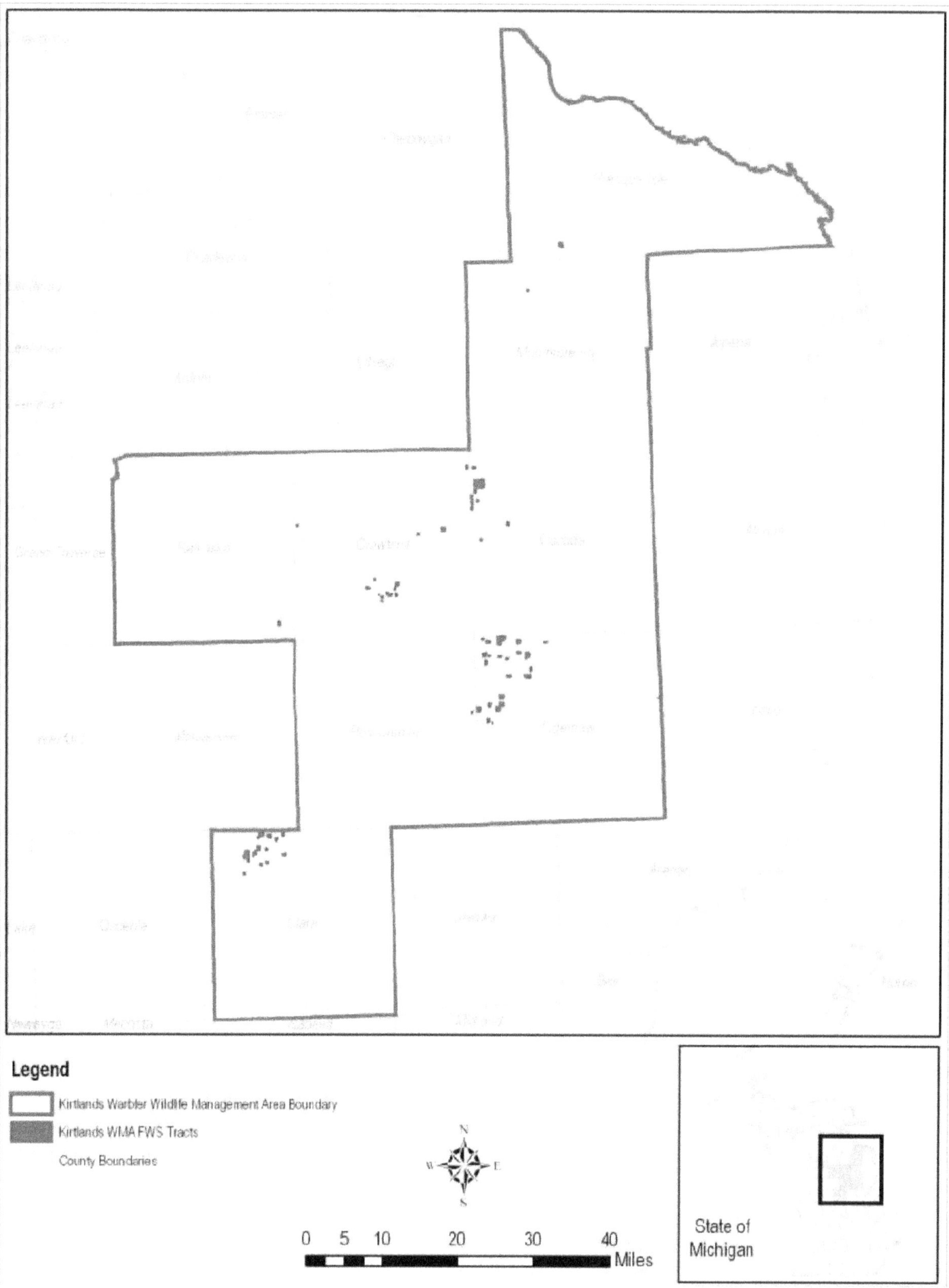

Legend

☐ Kirtlands Warbler Wildlife Management Area Boundary

▨ Kirtlands WMA FWS Tracts

County Boundaries

State of Michigan

0 5 10   20   30   40 Miles

1.4. Kirtland's Warbler WMA Goals

- Goal 1: Wildlife – Management will play an integral role in the recovery of the Kirtland's Warbler. Kirtland's Warbler WMA lands will support the broad array of wildlife species that are dependent on each seral stage of the jack pine ecosystems (from barrens to mature jack pine).

- Goal 2: Habitat – Manage habitat to support Kirtland's Warblers and associated wildlife species by providing near benchmark conditions across all seral stages of the jack pine ecosystem. Employ sound management practices that emulate patterns of structure and composition resulting from wildfire and other natural disturbances.

- Goal 3: People – Encourage the public to explore jack pine ecosystems and learn about its associated wildlife.

1.5. Vision Statement

The Kirtland's Warbler Wildlife Management Area will be managed to promote jack pine ecosystems that contribute to a sustainable population of Kirtland's Warblers and associated wildlife species. Lands will be actively managed to mimic historical disturbance regimes and resulting structural and compositional attributes, such as dense stands of jack pine with barren-like openings, snags and coarse woody debris. Research will be encouraged and the public will be invited to learn about jack pine ecosystems and the wildlife they support.

1.6. Decision Framework

The Regional Director for the Midwest Region (Region 3 of the U.S. Fish and Wildlife Service) will need to make two decisions based on this EA: (1) select an alternative future management, and (2) determine if the selected alternative is a major federal action significantly affecting the quality of the human environment, thus requiring preparation of an Environmental Impact Statement (EIS). The planning team has recommended Alternative 3 (Ecological Management and Land Ownership Con-

solidation) to the Regional Director. The CCP was developed for implementation based on this recommendation.

1.7. Authority, Legal Compliance, and Compatibility

The National Wildlife Refuge System includes federal lands managed primarily to provide habitat for a diversity of fish, wildlife and plant species. National wildlife refuges, and a few wildlife management areas such as Kirtland's Warbler WMA, are established under many different authorities and funding sources for a variety of purposes. The purposes for Kirtland's Warbler WMA were derived from the Endangered Species Act of 1973. Appendix D of the CCP contains a list of the key laws, orders and regulations that provide a framework for the proposed action.

1.8. Scoping of the Issues

The CCP planning process began in March 2006 and included internal discussions, a meeting with the Kirtland's Warbler Recovery Team, and a public open house. Please see Chapter 2 in the CCP for details of the issue scoping process.

1.8.1. Kirtland's Warbler WMA Issues, Concerns and Opportunities

The following list of issue topics was generated by internal scoping, the public open house sessions and program reviews.

1.8.1.1. Habitat Management

- *Forest Management:* How can we change current silvicultural practices to better emulate historic conditions?

- *Fire Management:* How can we restore prescribed fire to Kirtland's Warbler WMA lands?

- *Land Consolidation:* Kirtland's Warbler WMA parcels are inholdings within larger Michigan DNR parcels. Administration and habitat management would be more efficient if WMA parcels were consolidated into larger blocks by exchanging for other DNR or U.S. Forest Service lands.

1.8.1.2. Wildlife Management

- *Brown-headed Cowbird Management:* Are there ways other than trapping to deal with Brown-headed Cowbirds?

- *Kirtland's Warbler Census:* Will we be able to census birds each year?

- *Delisting:* What can we do from a land management standpoint to facilitate delisting of the species?

- *Biodiversity:* What can be done to improve habitat for native species other than the Kirtland's Warbler?

1.8.1.3. Public Use

- *Hunting:* Kirtland's Warbler WMA units are open to hunting per state regulations. Some hunting practices are generally not allowed on Refuge System lands such as baiting, construction of blinds, all-terrain vehicle (ATV) use, and using dogs to hunt bears.

- *Environmental Education:* If land exchange/consolidation occurs it would change outreach, interpretation, environmental education, staffing needs and opportunities.

- *Residential Development:* Rural housing construction causes direct habitat loss and complicates prescribed burning.

Chapter 2: Description of the Alternatives

2.1. Formulation of Alternatives

Based on the issues, concerns and opportunities we heard during the scoping process, the Planning Team developed three alternative management scenarios that could be used at Kirtland's Warbler WMA. These alternatives and the consequences of adopting each are presented in this Environmental Assessment. The alternatives were formulated under the assumption that staffing and budgets would remain constant or grow slowly throughout the life of the Plan.

The three management alternatives were developed to address most of the issues, concerns, and opportunities identified during the CCP planning process.

2.2. Management Alternatives

2.2.1. Alternative 1: Current Direction of Habitat Management (No Action)

The current management direction of Kirtland's Warbler WMA would be maintained under this alternative. For NEPA purposes, this is referred to as the "No Action" alternative, a misnomer as some changes will occur over the next 15 years. Nonetheless, in Alternative 1, intensive management of existing jack pine stands would continue to occur in close cooperation with the Michigan DNR, with the primary objective to produce dense jack pine plantations for Kirtland's Warbler breeding habitat. The WMA staff and Michigan DNR land managers would continue to monitor habitat prescription effects and make improvements in jack pine habitat management as it pertains primarily to Kirtland's Warbler. Public use would follow the current direction and be linked to uses of the surrounding state lands. Environmental education and outreach would be conducted primarily by other agencies and non-government organizations.

2.2.2. Alternative 2: Management from an Ecological Perspective

Alternative 2 would seek to make changes from the current high intensity habitat management that produces jack pine plantations for Kirtland's Warbler by trenching and planting. Future management would continue to involve the Michigan DNR, but would use a more ecologically broad and holistic jack pine ecosystem management approach based on benchmark conditions derived from jack pine stands regenerated by wildfire. This alternative would include management practices that place a greater emphasis on ecological integrity. Management would include emulating wildfire-produced jack pine stand composition and structural patterns that result in greater biodiversity. Timber harvests would try to better emulate wildfire-produced stand conditions and a range of regeneration options would be used, including prescribed fire when and where possible. An increased emphasis would also occur within law enforcement and visitor use. Enforcement of hunting regulations, trespass, and other violations would likely require more staff time and year-round presence. Visitor use would be facilitated by delineating the boundaries of some properties, developing interpretive signs and conducting outreach to surrounding communities.

2.2.3. Alternative 3: Ecological Management and Land Ownership Consolidation (Preferred Alternative)

Alternative 3 would seek to manage existing lands as suggested in Alternative 2, but would also explore land exchanges with the state (and possibly U.S. Forest Service) to consolidate DNR and WMA parcels. Proposed land exchanges would likely increase the total area of land managed for Kirtland's Warbler, as well as increase management efficiency by both federal and state agencies. Existing lands and any new lands acquired through exchange would be managed to benefit the Kirtland's Warbler and other native flora and fauna of jack pine ecosystems. However, the management of jack pine stands would shift away from plantations toward a more ecologically-based approach. As an example, if consolidation were to occur, and the Service obtained upland jack pine stands in the eastern Upper Peninsula, prescribed fire would be a more likely management tool. Guidelines for selection of lands for consolidation are found in Chapter 4 of the CCP.

2.2.4. Comparison of No Action and Preferred Alternatives

Under Alternative 1, the Current Direction or No Action Alternative, little change will occur overall in how Kirtland's Warbler WMA is managed and what wildlife species benefit from this management. The general management scheme will include clearcuts in jack pine-dominated stands, with follow-up treatment consisting of Michigan DNR trenching and hand-planting of jack pine seedlings. No land consolidation is proposed and Kirtland's Warbler WMA will continue to exist in a landscape of multiple ownerships. Those species for which habitats are being provided will continue to have their needs met by management actions. However, the small size of WMA tracts will preclude management actions that directly benefit many Regional Conservation Priority Species, especially those that inhabit only the largest patches of a habitat such as Upland Sandpiper and Northern Harrier.

Alternative 3, the Preferred Alternative, will result in substantially more change in how Kirtland's Warbler WMA is managed and what wildlife species benefit from these actions. These changes will likely result due to an increased focus on enhancing residual stand structure after trees are harvested (i.e., increasing the number of snags retained) and because land consolidation will allow the possible incorporation of prescribed fire into management of larger patches of jack pine. This is especially true if consolidation occurs within regional landscape with more public lands (e.g., the Upper Peninsula).

The management actions described in Alternative 3 would likely benefit more area-sensitive Regional Conservation Priority species and better emulate the natural biodiversity of jack pine ecosystems. However, relatively little shift in wildlife species composition would occur. Species shifts would occur if future land consolidation includes obtaining larger patches of xeric, jack pine-appropriate lands in the Upper Peninsula (Probst et al. 2003). Prescribed fire as a management tool would likely increase and this would allow for more heterogeneity in terms of resulting jack pine stand structure. Range-restricted wildlife species that would either be added to the species composition of Kirtland's Warbler WMA or increase in abundance include Sharp-tailed Grouse, Palm Warbler and Spruce Grouse. Species that would likely drop out include Prairie Warbler. Overall, a significant shift would occur if exchanges happen between existing land holdings in the northern Lower Peninsula and the eastern Upper Peninsula. Species to primarily benefit include those dependent on openland or grassland-shrubland-early successional forests.

Table 1: Comparison of Objectives and Environmental Consequences by Management Alternatives

Alternative 1: Current Direction of Habitat Management (No Action)	Alternative 2: Management from an Ecological Perspective	Alternative 3: Ecological Management and Land Ownership Consolidation (Preferred Alternative)
Goal 1: Wildlife – Management will play an integral role in the recovery of the Kirtland's Warbler. Kirtland's Warbler WMA lands will support the broad array of wildlife species that are dependent on each seral stage of the jack pine ecosystems (from barrens to mature jack pine).		
Objective 1.1: Continue to be an active partner in the Kirtland's Warbler recovery effort.	**Objective 1.1:** Same as Alternative 1	**Objective 1.1:** Same as Alternative 1.
Strategies: ■ Participate in the annual Kirtland's Warbler Census to aid in monitoring the population trends. ■ Work with Ecological Services to continue annual trapping efforts to remove Brown-headed Cowbirds from nesting areas and explore new ways to eliminate cowbirds parasitism of Kirtland's Warbler nests. ■ Coordinate harvest and regeneration of jack pine, on Kirtland's Warbler WMA lands with the, Michigan DNR to insure that the Services lands are contributing to the Kirtland's Warbler recovery effort. ■ Conduct and participate in research to better understand the ecology and management of Kirtland's Warbler populations.	*Strategies:* Same as Alternative 1	*Strategies:* Same as Alternative 1
Objective 1.2: By 2016, implement a monitoring program to track the presence, abundance, population trends, and/or habitat associations of Trust Resources and determine ways to emulate natural species diversity.	**Objective 1.2:** Same as Alternative 1.	Objective 1.2: Same as Alternative 1.
Strategies: ■ Determine the presence, abundance and habitat associations of Trust Resources currently using Kirtland's Warbler WMA lands. ■ Develop and implement a monitoring program to track population trends, and/or habitat associations of Trust Resources. *Continued on next page*	*Strategies:* ■ Same as Alternative 1 but including: ■ Hire a Refuge Manager to be located in the WMA. ■ Provide facilities for local staff including an office and storage areas.	*Strategies:* Same as Alternative 1

Table 1: Comparison of Objectives and Environmental Consequences by Management Alternatives

Alternative 1: Current Direction of Habitat Management (No Action)	Alternative 2: Management from an Ecological Perspective	Alternative 3: Ecological Management and Land Ownership Consolidation (Preferred Alternative)
Objective 1.2 Strategies: Continued • Conduct annual reviews of trends to determine if there are priorities for research or management. • If a Trust Resource research or management issue is identified, initiate action at the local level. If the issue goes beyond the boundary of the Kirtland's Warbler WMA, take lead role in coordinating with federal, state, and NGO partners to develop broader scale projects to resolve issues.		
Goal 2: Habitat – Manage habitat to support Kirtland's Warblers and associated wildlife species by providing near benchmark conditions across all seral stages of the jack pine ecosystem. Employ sound management practices that emulate patterns of structure and composition resulting from wildfire and other natural disturbances.		
Objective 2.1: Continue to manage jack pine stands in conjunction with Michigan DNR, but place greater emphasis on promoting ecological integrity within managed stands.	**Objective 2.1:** Continue to manage jack pine stands in conjunction with Michigan DNR, but place greater emphasis on promoting ecological integrity within managed stands. Emulate natural structural and compositional patterns of jack pine forests produced through wildfire.	**Objective 2.1:** Continue to manage jack pine stands in conjunction with Michigan DNR, but place greater emphasis on promoting ecological integrity within managed stands.
Strategies: • Work with federal, state and local officials to garner support for the use of prescribed fire in the management of jack pine to create Kirtland's Warbler nesting habitat. • Work with federal, state and local fire officials to employ prescribed fire as a management tool where it can be applied safely without risk to life and property. • Elsewhere, attempt to emulate the compositional and structural patterns of jack pine stands resulting from wildfire through mechanical treatments (i.e. timber sales). Place increased emphasis on maintaining "legacy" trees (e.g., large red and white pine, red and white oak, etc.) and providing more (and larger) standing snags and coarse woody debris. *Continued on next page*	*Strategies:* Same as Alternative 1	*Strategies:* Same as Alternative 1.

Table 1: Comparison of Objectives and Environmental Consequences by Management Alternatives

Alternative 1: Current Direction of Habitat Management (No Action)	Alternative 2: Management from an Ecological Perspective	Alternative 3: Ecological Management and Land Ownership Consolidation (Preferred Alternative)
Strategies: ■ Parcels that contain habitats other than jack pine will be managed to emulate patterns resulting from natural disturbances. ■ Develop research demonstration sites that exemplify ecologically-based jack pine management and illustrate how emulating natural conditions can provide multiple species benefits. ■ Develop a map and monitor spotted knapweed distribution within and near Kirtland's Warbler WMA parcels. Initiate removal if the species spreads into nesting areas.		
Not Applicable	Not Applicable	**Objective 2.2: Land Consolidation –** Within 5 years of completion of this CCP, develop a land consolidation plan for the Kirtland's Warbler WMA that maintains or increase habitat for the warbler and increase management efficiency for all agencies involved.
		Strategies: ■ Interagency team will follow land consolidation guidelines to establish priority exchange scenarios ■ Land appraisals, following federal and state guidelines, will be conducted on all lands identified for exchange.
Goal 3: People – Encourage the public to explore jack pine ecosystems and learn about its associated wildlife.		
Objective 3.1 – Hunting: Provide the public with opportunities to hunt on Kirtland's Warbler WMA lands in accordance with state and federal regulations.	**Objective 3.1 – Hunting:** Same as Alternative 1.	**Objective 3.1 – Hunting:** Same as Alternative 1.
Strategies: ■ Increase law enforcement on Service properties to ensure consistency with federal hunting regulations (e.g. no deer baiting, permanent blinds, bear hunting with dogs, and off-road vehicle use). ■ In cooperation with the Michigan DNR, produce maps to show the hunting public areas subject to federal regulations.	*Strategies:* Same as Alternative 1 but including: ■ Hire a Refuge Operations Specialist with law enforcement credentials. ■ Post the boundaries of WMA parcels with appropriate refuge signs. ■ Develop interpretive signs and place them at key locations.	*Strategies:* Same as Alternative 1.

Table 1: Comparison of Objectives and Environmental Consequences by Management Alternatives

Alternative 1: Current Direction of Habitat Management (No Action)	Alternative 2: Management from an Ecological Perspective	Alternative 3: Ecological Management and Land Ownership Consolidation (Preferred Alternative)
Objective 3.2 – Wildlife Observation, Wildlife Photography, Environmental Education and Environmental Interpretation: Within 5 years of approval of the plan, increase opportunities for wildlife observation and photography, environmental education and interpretation to correspond with an increase (from 2008 level) in WMA visitation. The level of knowledge about, and the positive attitude toward, the WMA will increase among visitors throughout the next 15 years.	**Objective 3.2 – Wildlife Observation, Wildlife Photography, Environmental Education and Environmental Interpretation:** Within 10 years of approval of the plan, increase opportunities for wildlife observation and photography, environmental education and interpretation to correspond with an increase (from 2008 level) in WMA visitation. The level of knowledge about, and the positive attitude toward, the WMA will increase among visitors throughout the next 15 years.	**Objective 3.2 – Wildlife Observation, Wildlife Photography, Environmental Education and Environmental Interpretation:** Same as Alternative 1.
Strategies: ■ Continue active support of the annual Kirtland's Warbler Festival and Tours. ■ Encourage wildlife-dependent activities on Kirtland's Warbler WMA lands by providing outreach materials, such as brochures and displays, at local public events and in community facilities.	*Strategies:* Same as Alternative 1 but including: ■ Hire a full-time Visitor Services specialist to increase community outreach and involvement.	*Strategies:* Same as Alternative 1.

Chapter 3: Affected Environment

This chapter includes a brief overview of the affected environments of Kirtland's Wildlife Management Area. More detail is contained in Chapter 3 of the CCP itself.

3.1. Introduction

Kirtland's Warbler WMA was established in 1980 in response to the need for more land dedicated to the restoration of this species. The U.S. Fish and Wildlife Service established the wildlife management area, in part, based on the recommendations of the Kirtland's Warbler Recovery Team. The original goal was to acquire 7,500 acres of land on which habitat would be managed for the benefit of Kirtland's Warbler. At present, the area contains 125 separate tracts totaling 6,684 acres. While management for Kirtland's Warbler is paramount, the WMA provides habitat for a diversity of wildlife species, both migratory and non-migratory.

3.2. Archeological and Cultural Values

No prehistoric resources or historic resources eligible for the National Register of Historic Places have been found on Kirtland's Warbler WMA properties. Please refer to Chapter 3 of the CCP for more details.

3.3. Social and Economic Context

Please see Chapter 3 of the CCP for more details.

3.4. Natural Resources

3.4.1. Habitats

The physical characteristics of the Kirtland's Warbler WMA are consistent with most of the northern half of the Lower Peninsula of Michigan. Topographically, the land is flat to gently rolling. Landforms are glacially derived. In terms of physiography and land classification, the majority of the stands (94 percent) are in the Highplains Landtype Association with 6 percent in the Presque Isle Landtype Association. Three soil associations dominate the tracts namely Grayling – Graycalm - Au Gres (35 percent), Rubicon – Grayling - Croswell (34 percent), and Grayling – Rubicon - Au Gres (21 percent). Heavy sands are a major component in all three soil associations.

3.4.1.1. Wetlands

Approximately 2 percent of the Kirtland's Warbler WMA or 137 ac is characterized by wetland ecosystems and 0.6 percent is classified as lakes. No detailed inventories or research have been conducted within these habitat types, however.

3.4.1.2. Uplands

According to the contract work completed by Goebel et al. (2007), 41 percent of the stands (2,695 acres) are between 5-23 years old, while 14 percent (959 acres) are less than 5 years old and 45 percent (2,298 acres) are greater than 23 years old. It is important to note that many of the stands have multiple cohorts; to determine the age of each stand the most extensive cohort was considered indicative of the overall stand age.

Seventeen overstory (stems greater than 4 inches dbh) tree species have been found at Kirtland's Warbler WMA. Jack pine, red pine, scarlet oak, trembling aspen, black cherry, black oak, northern red oak, and bigtooth aspen are the most common over-

Table 2: Bird Species Stongly Associated with Young (< 5 years old), KW (5-23 years old), and old (> 23 years old) Stands of the KWWMA

Young (< 5 years old)	KW (5-23 years old)	Old (> 23 years old)
Indigo Bunting***	Kirtland's Warbler***	Eastern Wood-Pewee***
Eastern Bluebird***	Nashville Warbler***	Hermit Thrush***
Field Sparrow***	Eastern Towhee***	Ovenbird***
Lincoln's Sparrow***	Brown Thrasher**	Rose-breasted Grosbeak***
Black-billed Cuckoo*	Alder Flycatcher**	Red-breasted Nuthatch***
		Red-eyed Vireo***
		Black-capped Chickadee**
		Chipping Sparrow**
		Mourning Dove*

*P < 0.05; ** P < 0.01; *** P < 0.001.
Table 2 provides the results of a statistical procedure that assigns species to each of the three stand ages based on frequency of encounters. It also only shows species whose *P*-value is <0.05. Some species are also highly associated with these stands, but at greater *P*-values.

story species. Less common species include eastern white pine, red maple, balsam fir, green ash, black ash, white spruce, northern pin oak and fire cherry.

3.4.2. Wildlife

3.4.2.1. Birds

The loss of landscape structural diversity in jack pine ecosystems (from barrens to forests) can influences ecoregional populations of many bird species. Whereas jack pine plantations provide food and shelter for a certain suite of species, other jack pine ecosystems offer habitat for a different suite of birds, many of which are of conservation priority. Species that utilize mature jack stands include Black-backed Woodpecker, Spruce Grouse, and Olive-sided Flycatcher. In young jack pine stands and open areas of pine barrens, many openland (grassland and shrubland) birds of conservation concern breed. Species found in the early successional stages of jack pine ecosystems include (of course) Kirtland's Warbler, Palm Warbler, Black-billed Cuckoo, Brown Thrasher, Eastern Towhee, and Nashville Warbler. American Kestrel, Northern Harrier, Upland Sandpiper, and Clay-colored Sparrow can be found in the larger, more open areas.

3.4.2.2. Mammals

Based on state-wide distribution patterns (Kurta 2001), there are approximately 52 extant mammal species possible within the Kirtland's Warbler WMA (Appendix C). However, range expansion of some species is likely to occur soon. For instance, although not prevalent within the Lower Peninsula of Michigan now, the gray wolf is likely to become more common in the future. Species of high public interest include river otter, beaver, snowshoe hare, and white-tailed deer.

3.4.2.3. Fish

No fish surveys have been conducted. Only a few small water bodies are found on WMA parcels.

3.4.2.4. Reptiles and Amphibians

Based on state-wide distribution patterns (multiple authors), 36 species of herptofauna possibly exist within the Kirtland's Warbler WMA and many of these species are Conservation Priority Species (Appendix C). Much more inventory work is required at the Kirtland's Warbler WMA and much of this work should be done as part of applied research.

3.4.2.5. Threatened and Endangered Species

Aside from Kirtland's Warbler, no other current federally-listed species is known to use the Kirtland's Warbler WMA tracts. The gray wolf, a federally listed endangered species, was delisted in 2007 but their status is subject to ongoing court actions. It is unlikely that the Kirtland's Warbler WMA tracts are used by wolves during any time of the year as this species is at best rare in the northern

Lower Peninsula. The Michigan DNR conducts aerial surveys for the wolves all year long and reports the information.

3.5. Visitor Services

Although most statistics regarding the use of Kirtland's Warbler WMA for Visitor Services are lacking, the WMA provides opportunities for wildlife-dependent activities such as hunting, wildlife observation, wildlife photography, environmental education and environmental interpretation. Please see Chapter 3 of the CCP for more detail on visitor services at Kirtland's Warbler WMA.

Chapter 4: Environmental Consequences

4.1. Effects Common to All Alternatives

Specific environmental and social impacts of implementing each alternative are compared in Table 1 within the broad categories of wildlife, habitat and people. However, several potential effects will be very similar under each alternative and are summarized below:

4.1.1. Environmental Justice

Executive Order 12898 "Federal Actions to Address Environmental Justice in Minority Populations and Low-Income Populations" was signed by President Clinton on February 11, 1994. Its purpose was to focus the attention of federal agencies on the environmental and human health conditions of minority and low-income populations with the goal of achieving environmental protection for all communities. The Order directed federal agencies to develop environmental justice strategies to aid in identifying and addressing disproportionately high and adverse human health or environmental effects of their programs, policies, and activities on minority and low-income populations. The Order is also intended to promote nondiscrimination in federal programs substantially affecting human health and the environment, and to provide minority and low-income communities access to public information and participation in matters relating to human health or the environment.

None of the management alternatives described in this EA would disproportionately place any adverse environmental, economic, social, or health impacts on minority and low-income populations. The percentage of minorities in the northern Lower Peninsula of Michigan is lower than in Michigan (and much lower than the United States) as a whole. Average incomes and poverty rates within the counties is comparable to other rural counties in the state. Public use activities that would be offered under each of the alternatives would be available to any visitor regardless of race, ethnicity or income level.

4.1.2. Climate Change Impacts

The U.S. Department of the Interior issued an order in January 2001 requiring federal agencies, under its direction, that have land management responsibilities to consider potential climate change impacts as part of long range planning endeavors. The increase of carbon dioxide (CO_2) within the earth's atmosphere has been linked to the gradual rise in surface temperature commonly referred to as global warming. In relation to comprehensive conservation planning for national wildlife refuges, carbon sequestration constitutes the primary climate-related impact to be considered in planning. The U.S. Department of Energy's "Carbon Sequestration Research and Development" defines carbon sequestration as "...the capture and secure storage of carbon that would otherwise be emitted to or remain in the atmosphere."

Please refer to Chapter 3 of the CCP for more detail on potential climate change impacts in Northern Michigan and the Great Lakes Region.

4.1.3. Cultural Resources

The USFWS is responsible for managing archeological and historic sites found on national wildlife refuges. There are no identified cultural resources on Kirtland's Warbler WMA. However, there may be cultural resources awaiting discovery. Under each alternative evaluated in this EA, WMA management would ensure compliance with relevant federal laws and regulations, particularly Section 106 of the National Historic Preservation Act. Prior to all habitat and facility projects, appropriate efforts will be made to identify cultural resources within the area of potential impact by contacting the Regional Historic Preservation Officer.

4.1.4. Other Common Effects

None of the alternatives would have more than negligible, or at most minor effects on soils, topography, noise levels, land use patterns, transportation and traffic, waste management, human health and safety, or visual resources.

4.2. Cumulative Impacts Analysis

"Cumulative environmental impacts" refer to effects that result from the incremental impact of the proposed action when added to other past, present and reasonably foreseeable future actions, regardless of what agency (federal or nonfederal) or person undertakes such other actions. Cumulative impacts can result from individually minor but collectively significant actions taking place over a period of time. Land parcels under the jurisdiction of the Kirtland's Warbler WMA are relatively small and scattered over eight counties. No cumulative impacts have been identified for actions suggested in this EA.

Chapter 5: List of Preparers

Refuge Staff:

- Tracy Casselman, Refuge Manager
- Greg Corace, Forester

Regional Office Staff:

- Gary Muehle nhardt, W ildlife Biologist/Ref - uge Planner, Region 3, USFWS
- Gabriel DeAles sio, Biol ogist-GIS, Region 3, USFWS
- John   Dobrovolny, Regional Historian, Region 3, USFWS (retired)
- Jane Hodgin s, T echnical   Writer/Editor, Region 3, USFWS

Chapter 6: Consultation and Coordination with Stakeholders

The Refuge and Regional Planning staffs have conducted extensive consultation and coordination over two years with stakeholders in developing the CCP and EA for Kirtland's Warbler WMA. In the course of scoping and other meetings, the Service consulted with more than two dozen individuals representing Michigan DNR, conservation organizations, neighboring communities, and other stakeholders. See Chapter 2 of the CCP for a more detailed description of the process.

Appendix B: Glossary

Appendix B: Glossary

Alternative

A s et of obj ectives and strateg ies needed to achieve refuge goals and the desired future con- dition.

Biological Diversity

The variety of life forms and its processes, includ- ing the variety of living organisms, the genetic differences among them, and the comm unities and ecosystems in which they occur.

Compatible Use

A wildlife-dependent recreational use, o r any other use on a refuge that will not materially interfere with or detr act from the fulfillment of the mission of the S ervice or the purpos es of the refuge.

Comprehensive Conservation Plan

A document that describes the desired future conditions of the refuge, and s pecifies manage- ment actions to achieve refuge goals and the mis- sion of the National Wildlife Refuge System.

Conservation

Active ma nagement to mainta in ex isting condi- tions, more or less.

Cultural Resources

"Those parts of the physical environment -- natu- ral and built -- that have cultural va lue to some kind of soci ocultural group ... [and] those non- material human soc ial institu tions...." Cultural resources include historic sites , archeolog ical sites and associated artifacts , sacred sites, tradi- tional cultural properties, cultural item s (human remains, funerar y obj ects, s acred objects, and objects of cultural patrim ony), and buildings and structures.

Ecosystem

A dynamic and interrelated complex of plant and animal communities and their associated non-liv- ing environment.

Ecosystem Approach

A strategy or plan to protect and restore the nat- ural function, str ucture, and species composition of an ecosystem, recognizing that all components are interrelated.

Ecosystem Management

Management of an ecosys tem that includes all ecological, social and ec onomic components that make up the whole of the system.

Endangered Species

Any spec ies of plant or ani mal defined through the Endangered Species A ct as being in danger of extinction thro ughout all or a significant por- tion of its range, and published in the F ederal Register.

Environmental Assessment

A systematic analysis to determine if proposed actions would result in a si gnificant effect on the quality of the environment.

Extirpation

The local extinction of a spe cies that is no longer found in a loca lity or countr y, but exists else - where in the world.

Goals

Descriptive s tatements of desired future condi - tions.

High Quality Recreation

Wildlife-dependent recreational program s that meet criteria defined in Section 1.6 of 605 FW 1.

Interjurisdictional Fish

Fish that occur in waters under the jurisdiction of one or m ore states, for which there is an inter- state fishery management plan or which migrates between the waters under the jurisdiction of two or more states bordering on the Great Lakes.

Issue

Any unsettled matter that requires a manag e- ment decision. F or example, a resource manag e- ment probl em, concer n, a threat to natural resources, a conflict in uses, or in the presence of an undesirable resource condition.

Landbirds

All birds that inhabit non-wetland habitats.

National Wildlife Refuge System

All lands, waters, and interes ts therein administered by the U.S. F ish and Wildlife Ser vice as
wildlife refuges, wildlife ranges, wildlife management areas, water fowl production areas, and
other areas for the protection and conservation of
fish, wildlife and plant resources.

Objectives

A concise statement of what we want to achieve.
The statement i s speci fic, measurable, ac hiev-
able, results oriented, and time-fixed.

Preferred Alternative

The Ser vice's selected alternative identified in
the environmental assess ment and fully devel -
oped in the Comprehensive Conservation Plan.

Preservation

Passive managem ent that a llows patter ns to
develop without intervention.

Restoration

Active managem ent to return patter ns or processes to a measured, pre-European condition.

Scoping

A process for deter mining the s cope of issues to
be addres sed by a comprehensive conser vation
plan and f or id entifying th e significant issues.
Involved in the s coping process are federal, s tate
and loca l agen cies; priv ate organizations; and
individuals.

Species

A distin ctive ki nd of pla nt or an imal havi ng di s-
tinguishable chara cteristics, and that can i nter-
breed and produce young. A categor y of
biological classification.

Strategies

A general approach or specific actions to achieve
objectives.

Threatened Species

Those plant or anim al species likely to become
endangered species throughout all of or a signifi -
cant portion of their range within the foreseeable
future. A plant or animal identified and defined in
accordance with the 1973 End angered Species
Act and published in the Federal Register.

Trust Resources

Trust resources are those resources for which the
Service has been given specific respons ibilities
under federal law. These include migratory birds,
interjurisdictional fish es (fish speci es t hat may
cross state lines), federally listed threatened or
endangered species, some marine mamm als, and
lands owned by the Service.

Undertaking:

"A proj ect, activity, or pro gram funded in whole
or in part under the direct or indirect jurisdiction
of a F ederal agency, in cluding th ose ca rried out
by or on behalf of a Federal agency; those carried
out with F ederal financial a ssistance; those
requiring a F ederal per mit, li cense or
approval...," i.e., all Federal actions.

Vegetation

Plants in general, or the sum total of the plant life
in an area.

Vegetation Type

A category of land based on potential or existing
dominant plant species of a particular area.

Waterbirds

This general categor y in cludes all bi rds that
inhabit lakes , marshes, streams and other wet -
lands at some point during the year . The group
includes all waterfowl, such as ducks, geese, and
swans, and other birds su ch as loons, rails,
cranes, herons, egrets, ibis, cormorants, pelicans,
shorebirds an d pas serines th at nest and rely on
wetland vegetation.

Watershed

The entire la nd area that collects and drai ns
water into a stream or stream system.

Wetland

Areas suc h as lakes, marshes, and stream s that
are inundated by sur face or ground water for a
long enough period of time each year to support,
and that do support under natural conditions,
plants and animals that require saturated or sea-
sonally saturated soils.

Wildlife-dependent Recreational Use

A use of a refuge that involves hunting, fishing,
wildlife observation and photography, or environmental education and interpretation, as identified
in the National Wildlife Refuge System Improvement Act of 1997.

Wildlife Diversity

A measure of the number of wildlife species in an
area.

Appendix C: Species Lists

List of Woody Plant Species Found on Kirtland's Warbler Wildlife Management Area [1]

Scientific Name	Common Name
Abies balsamea	Balsam Fir
Acer rubrum	Red Maple
Alnus incana	Tag Alder
Amelanchier spp.	Serviceberry spp.
Betula spp.	Birch spp.
Crataegus spp.	Hawthorn spp.
Fraxinus americana	White Ash
F. nigra	Black Ash
F. pennsylvanica	Green Ash
Hamamelis virginiana	Witch-hazel
Pinus banksiana	Jack Pine
Picea glauca	White Spruce
Pinus resinosa	Red Pine
P. sylvestris	Scots Pine
P. strobus	White Pine
Populus grandidentata	Bigtooth Aspen
P.t remuloides	Trembling Aspen
Prunus pennsylvanica	Pin Cherry
P.s erotina	Black Cherry
P. virginiana	Choke Cherry
Quercus alba	White Oak
Q. coccinea	Scarlet Oak
Q. ellipsoidalis	Northern Pin Oak
Q. rubra	Northern Red Oak
Q. velutina	Black Oak

1. *Goebel et al. (2007)*

Birds of Kirtland's Warbler Wildlife Management Area[1]

Common Name	Scientific Name	Nest[2]		Special Status		
		LOC1	LOC2	Region 3 Conservation Priorities	Regional Forester Sensitive	Michigan Special Animal
Alder Flycatcher	*Empidonax alnorum*	SH				
American Crow	*Corvus brachyrhynchos*	DT	SH			
American Goldfinch	*Carduelis tristis*	SH	TR			
American Redstart	*Setophaga ruticilla*	DT	SH			
American Robin	*Turdus migratorius*	DT	CT			
Barred Owl	*Strix varia*	DT	SH			
Black-billed Cuckoo1	*Coccyzus erythropthalmus*	DT	SN	✓		
Black-capped Chickadee	*Poecile atricapillus*	SN				
Blue Jay	*Cyanocitta cristata*	DT	GR			
Blue-headed Vireo	*Vireo solitarius*	CT				
Brown Creeper	*Certhia americana*	CT	DT			
Brown Thrasher	*Toxostoma rufum*	SH	GR			
Brown-headed Cowbird	*Molothrus ater*	SH	GR			
Cedar Waxwing	*Bombycilla cedrorum*	DT	CT			
Chipping Sparrow	*Spizella passerina*	CT	DT			
Clay-colored Sparrow	*Spizella pallida*	DT	CT			
Common Grackle	*Quiscalus quiscula*	GR				
Common Nighthawk	*Chordeiles minor*	CL	CT			
Common Raven	*Corvus corax*	GR				
Common Yellowthroat	*Geothlypis trichas*	SH				
Eastern Bluebird	*Sialia sialis*	SN				
Eastern Kingbird	*Tyrannus tyrannus*	DT	SH			
Eastern Phoebe	*Sayornis phoebe*	BR	CL			
Eastern Towhee	*Pipilo erythrophthalmus*	GR	SH			
Eastern Wood-Pewee	*Contopus virens*	DT				
Field Sparrow1	*Spizella pusilla*	GR	SH	✓		
Golden-crowned Kinglet	*Regulus satrapa*	DT	SN			
Great Crested Flycatcher	*Myiarchus crinitus*	CT				

Birds of Kirtland's Warbler Wildlife Management Area[1]

Common Name	Scientific Name	Nest[2]		Special Status		
		LOC1	LOC2	Region 3 Conservation Priorities	Regional Forester Sensitive	Michigan Special Animal
Hairy Woodpecker	*Picoides villosus*	DT	SN			
Hermit Thrush	*Catharus guttatus*	GR	TR			
House Wren	*Troglodytes aedon*	DT	SN			
Indigo Bunting	*Passerina cyanea*	SH	TR			
Kirtland's Warbler	*Dendroica kirtlandii*	GR		✓		✓
Least Flycatcher	*Empidonax minimus*	DT	SH			
Lincoln's Sparrow	*Melospiza lincolnii*	GR				
Mourning Dove	*Zenaida macroura*	TR	GR			
Mourning Warbler	*Oporornis philadelphia*	GR				
Nashville Warbler	*Vermivora ruficapilla*	CT				
Northern Flicker	*Colaptes auratus*	GR		✓		
Ovenbird	*Seiurus aurocapilla*	SN				
Pine Warbler	*Dendroica pinus*	GR				
Red-breasted Nuthatch	*Sitta vireo*	CT				
Red-eyed Vireo	*Vireo olivaceus*	DT	SH			
Red-tailed Hawk	*Buteo jamaicensis*	CT				
Red-winged Blackbird	*Agelaius phoeniceus*	SH	DT			
Rose-breasted Grosbeak	*Pheucticus ludovicianus*	DT	CL			
Scarlet Tanager	*Piranga olivacea*	RD				
Slate-colored Junco	*Junco hyemalis*	GR	BK			
Song Sparrow	*Melospiza melodia*	DT	CT			
Spotted Sandpiper	*Actitis macularius*	GR	SH			
Tree Swallow	*Tachycineta bicolor*	CT	DT			
Turkey Vulture	*Cathartes aura*	GR				
Upland Sandpiper	*Bartramia longicauda*	SN		✓	✓	
Vesper Sparrow	*Pooecetes gramineus*	CL	SN		✓	
White-breasted Nuthatch	*Sitta carolinensis*	GR				
White-throated Sparrow	*Zonotrichia albicollis*	GR				

Birds of Kirtland's Warbler Wildlife Management Area[1]

Common Name	Scientific Name	Nest[2]		Special Status		
		LOC1	LOC2	Region 3 Conservation Priorities	Regional Forester Sensitive	Michigan Special Animal
Wild Turkey	*Meleagris gallopavo*	DT				
Wilson's Snipe	*Gallinago delicata*	GR				
Yellow-bellied Sapsucker	*Sphyrapicus varius*	GR	SH			
Yellow-rumped Warbler	*Dendroica coronata*	DT				

1. *Birds of Kirtland's Warbler Wildlife Management Area recorded during point counts within KWWMA parcels in June and July 2006.*
2. *The 'NEST' columns provide alphabetic code for the primary (LOC1) and secondary (LOC2) nest site locations commonly utilized by the species (Ehrlich et al. 1988); the designations are as follows: BK – bank, GR – ground, BR – bridge, RD – reeds, CL – cliff, SH – shrub, CT – coniferous tree, SN – snag, DT – deciduous tree, TR – tree*

Possible Mammal Species of Kirtland's Warbler Wildlife Management Area

Common Name	Scientific Name	Habitat(s)[1]	Habitat(s)[2]	Special Status		
				Region 3 Conservation Priorities	Regional Forester Sensitive	Michigan Special Animal
Opossum	*Didelphis virginiana*	Deciduous woods near stream or lake, semi open country brushy fenelines, drainage ditches, and swamp borders	MDF, W DF, SUP			
Northern Short-tailed Shrew	*Blarina brevicauda*	Moist environments with extensive herbaceous cover or a thick layer of litter	WDF, M DF, WMF, WCF, SWE			
Masked Shrew	*Sorex cinereus*	Moist woodlots containing abundant plant cover, thick leaf litter, and decaying logs. Can include overgrown fields, alder thicket, cedar swamps, weedy fencerows, grassy marshes, and sphagnum bogs	MDF, W DF, PAS, GRA, HAY, SWE			
Water Shrew	*Sorex palustris*	Sluggish stream, bog or seasonal pond, but optimal habitat is small forest lined stream, with fast flowing water, and plenty of cover provided by undercut banks, jumbled rocks, downed trees, and other debris.	MDF, MMF, MCF, SHO		✓	
Pygmy Shrew	*Sorex hoyi*	Deciduous woods, coniferous forests, regenerating clear-cuts, grassy fields, swamps, bogs, and floodplains. Most live in boreal habitats with extensive ground cover.	DDF, MDF, DMF, D CF, GRA, SUP, SWE			
Star-nosed Mole	*Condylura cristata*	Wet saturated soils and frequents the borders of swamps, lakes, streams, or isolated areas of poor drainage.	WDF, WMF, WCF, SWE, OWE			
Eastern Mole	*Scalopus aquaticus*	Damp soils of forests, fields, pastures and lawns	DCF, DDF, DMF, GRA, PAS, RES			
Little Brown Bat	*Myotis lucifugus*	Buildings	RES			
Northern Bat	*Myotis septentrionalis*	Silver maples, hollow green ash, underneath loose bark of dead trees	DDF		✓	
Hoary Bat	*Lasiurus cinereus*	Any tree with dense shade, seclusion, and clear space below the roost	DDF, MDF, DMF, MMF, DCF, MCF			
Red Bat	*Lasiurus borealis*	Leafy trees (elms, maples) or in conifers	DDF, MDF, DMF, D CF, MCF			
Big Brown Bat	*Eptesicus fuscus*	Buildings	RES			
Silver-haired Bat	*Lasionycteris noctivagans*	Fond of willows, maple or ash	DDF, MDF			

Possible Mammal Species of Kirtland's Warbler Wildlife Management Area

Common Name	Scientific Name	Habitat(s)[1]	Habitat(s)[2]	Special Status		
				Region 3 Conservation Priorities	Regional Forester Sensitive	Michigan Special Animal
Snowshoe Hare	*Lepus americanus*	Heavily forested areas with dense understory. Thrives in coniferous and mixed woods including cedar bogs and spruce swamps.	DMF, MMF, MCF, DCF			
Woodchuck	*Marmota monax*	Rolling farmland interspersed with grassy pastures, small woodlots, and brushy fencelines	OLD, GRA, PAS, HAY			
Eastern Cottontail	*Sylvilagus floridanus*	Herbaceous vegetation abounds and potential shelter exists from brush piles, shrubby thickets, or weedy fencerows.	SUP, OLD, GRA, PAS, HAY			
Fox Squirrel	*Sciurus niger*	Deciduous trees in areas that lack a well-developed understory. Frequents woodlots, forest-field edges	DDF, MDF, OLD			
Red Squirrel	*Tamiasciurus hudsonicus*	Extensive stands of evergreen trees or mixed Coniferous/deciduous woodland	DCF, M CF, DMF, MMF			
Thirteen-lined Ground Squirrel	*Spermophilus tridecemlineatus*	Open areas with short grass	GRA			
Eastern Chipmunk	*Tamis striatus*	Open deciduous forests where stumps, logs, rocky outcrops Ultimate habitat beech maple forest	DDF, MDF			
Northern Flying Squirrel	*Glaucomys sabrinus*	Mixed forests with mature deciduous and coniferous trees. Also frequents pure stands of either type.	DMF, MMF			
Southern Flying Squirrel	*Glaucomys volans*	Open deciduous woodlots with few shrubby thickets scattered among mature trees.	DDF, MDF			
Beaver	*Castor canadensis*	Slow-moving streams or lakes bordered by young forests containing aspen, willow, or alder.	SHO			
House Mouse	*Mus musculus*	Buildings, cultivated fields, fencerows, wooded areas (around buildings)	RES, HAY			
Norway Rat	*Rattus norvegicus*	Buildings, cultivated fields.	RES, HAY			
Woodland Deer Mouse	*Peromyscus maniculatus gracilis*	Forested habitats, shrubby areas, regenerating clear-cuts, and recent burns.	SUP, DCF, MCF,D DF, MDF,D MF, MMF			
Woodland Vole	*Microtus pinetorum*	Forests of oak, maple, and beech are preferred, but present in all forest types and orchards	DCF, M CF, DDF, MDF, DMF, MMF			✓

Possible Mammal Species of Kirtland's Warbler Wildlife Management Area

Common Name	Scientific Name	Habitat(s)[1]	Habitat(s)[2]	Special Status		
				Region 3 Conservation Priorities	Regional Forester Sensitive	Michigan Special Animal
Red-backed Vole	*Clethrionomys gapperi*	Coniferous forests are preferred, deciduous or mixed coniferous/ deciduous woods acceptable with standing water nearby.	MDF,MMF, MCF, SWE, SHO			
White-footed Mouse	*Peromyscus leucopus*	Deciduous woodlands, where herbaceous cover is moderate and rocks and logs are abundant.	DDF, MDF			
Meadow Vole	*Microtus pennsylvanicus*	Moist, grassy fields and also frequents marshes and bog thick with greases, sedges and rushes.	SWE, OLD, OWE			
Muskrat	*Ondatra zibethicus*	Slow-moving streams, lakes, ponds, and especially marshes.	OWA, OWE			
Southern Bog Lemming	*Synaptomys cooperi*	Old fields, clear-cuts, shrubby locations, and upland woods. Frequents wet forested sites dominated by spruce, cedar, or tamarack, as well as more open sphagnum bogs.	MDF,W DF, MMF, WMF, MC, WCF, ORA, SUP, SWE			
Woodland Jumping Mouse	*Napaeozapus insignis*	Cool moist forests, with spruce-fir and hemlock hardwood associations but also in pure deciduous stands. Must be littered with rocks, logs, and stumps coated with a lush growth of ferns, grasses, and other.	MDF, MMF, MCF			
Meadow Jumping Mouse	*Zapus hudsonius*	Variety of habitats. Fallow fields, woodland edges, shrubby thickets. Abundant in moist sites containing lush growth of grasses and forbs (damp meadows, streamside vegetation, and marsh borders)	SWE, GRA, PAS, SHO			
Porcupine	*Erethizon dorsatum*	Deciduous and coniferous woodlands of stands containing pine and hemlock.	DDF, MDF, DMF, MMF, DCF, MCF			
Coyote	*Canis latrans*	Prairies, brushy area, wooded edges	DDF, MDF, DMF, MMF, DCF,M CF, PAS, G RA, HAY			
Gray Fox	*Urocyon cinereoargenteus*	In wooded swamps and in bottomland forests where woodlands and farmlands are mixed	DDF, MDF, DMF, MMF, DCF, WCF			
Red Fox	*Vulpes vulpes*	Open country with reliable cover nearby, frequents forest-field edges, brushy fencelines and wooded borders of streams or lakes.	DDF, OLD, PAS, H AY			

Possible Mammal Species of Kirtland's Warbler Wildlife Management Area

Common Name	Scientific Name	Habitat(s)[1]	Habitat(s)[2]	Special Status		
				Region 3 Conservation Priorities	Regional Forester Sensitive	Michigan Special Animal
Black Bear	*Ursus americanus*	Dense coniferous or deciduous woods having a thick understory.	DDF, MDF, DMF, MMF, DCF, MCF		✓	
Raccoon	*Procyon lotor*	In or near wooded areas, often near a stream or pond. More abundant in hardwood stands than coniferous	DDF, MDF, DMF, MMF			
Mink	*Mustela vison*	Streams, ponds, lakes with at least some brushy or rocky cover.	OWA, SWA			
Short-tailed Weasel	*Mustela erminea*	Open forests, riparian woodlands, and shrubby fencerows.				
Long-tailed Weasel	*Mustela frenata*	Forest-field edges, brushy fencelines, and wooded areas with shrubby cover	DDF, MDF, OLD, PAS, SHO			
Least Weasel	*Mustela nivalis*	Open forest, riparian edges, pastures, old fields and occasionally mature forests	OLD, DDF, DMF, D CF, PAS			
Striped Skunk	*Mephitis mephitis*	Mix of forests, fields, and wooded ravines.	HAY, PAS, DDF, MDF, DMF, MMF, DCF, DMF			
River Otter	*Lutra canadensis*	Clean, moderately deep streams, ponds, lakes.	OWA		✓	
Badger	*Taxidae taxus*	Grasslands, open fields, and pastures.	GRA, PAS, HAY		✓	
Marten	*Martes americana*	Closed coniferous woodlands underlain by a lush growth of shrubs and forbs and appears less in mixed stands.	DCF, MCF		✓	
Bobcat	*Lynx rufus*	Lies in coniferous and mixed deciduous/coniferous woods. Readily occupies wooded swamps close to riparian forest	DMF, MMF, DCF, MCF		✓	
White-tailed Deer	*Odocoileus virginianus*	Open forest environments interspersed with meadows, woodland clearings or farmland.				
Elk	*Cervus elaphus*	Open forest that includes meadows and woodland clearings				

1. *Habitat information obtained from: Kurta (2001).*

2. *Habitat Definitions (Brewer et al. 1991): DDF= Dry Deciduous Forest or Savanna; MDF= Mesic Deciduous Forest; WDF= Wet Deciduous Forest; DMF= Dry Mixed Forest or Savanna; MMF= Mesic Mixed Forest; WMF=Wet Mixed Forest; DCF=Dry Coniferous Forest; MCF=Mesic Coniferous Forest; WCF= Wet Coniferous Forest; SUP= Shrub Uplands; SWE= Shrub Wetland; OLD= Old Field; GRA= Grassland ; PAS= Pasture; HAY= Hayfield; OWE=Open Wetland; SHO= Shoreland; OWA= Open Water*

Possible Herptofaunal Species of Kirtland's Warbler WMA Based on Distribution Patterns in Michigan

Common Name	Scientific Name	Habitat(s)[1]	Special Status		
			Region 3 Conservation Priorities	Regional Forester Sensitive	Michigan Special Animal
Northern Water Snake	*Nerodia sipedon sipedon*	Ephemeral wetlands, forests, agricultural areas			
Northern Red-bellied Snake	*Storeria occipitomaculata occipitomaculata*	Permanent wetlands, rivers and streams, forests, grasslands and savannas, agricultural areas, urban areas			
Butler's Garter Snake	*Thamnophis butleri*	Open grasslands and prairies			
Eastern Garter Snake	*Thamnophis sirtalis sirtalis*	Ephemeral wetlands, permanent wetlands, rivers and streams, forests, grasslands and savannas, caves and springs, agricultural areas, urban areas			
Northern Ribbon Snake	*Thamnophis sauritus*	Riparian areas, streams, ponds, bogs and swamps			
Northern Brown Snake	*Storeria dekayi*	Bogs, swamps, marshes, moist woodlands and hillsides			
Eastern Hognose Snake	*Heterodon platyrhinos*	Sandy areas			
Northern Ringneck Snake	*Diadophis punctatus edwardsi*	Rivers and streams, forests, grasslands and savannas			
Eastern Smooth Green Snake	*Opheodrys vernalis*	Forests, grasslands and savannas			
Eastern Milk Snake	*Lampropeltis triangulum*	Fields, riverbottoms, rocky hillsides, woodlands			
Eastern Massasauga	*Sistrurus catenatus*	Wet prairies, bogs, swamps	✓	✓	✓
Snapping Turtle	*Chelydra serpentina*	Ephemeral wetlands, permanent wetlands, rivers and streams, grasslands and savannas, agricultural areas			
Wood Turtle	*Clemmys insculpta*	Rivers and streams, forests, agricultural areas		✓	✓
Spotted Turtle	*Clemmys guttata*	Shallow water bodies, marshy meadows, bogs, and swamps		✓	✓
Blanding's Turtle	*Emydoidea blandingii*	Ephemeral wetlands, permanent wetlands, rivers and streams, grasslands and savannas, agricultural areas		✓	✓

Possible Herptofaunal Species of Kirtland's Warbler WMA Based on Distribution Patterns in Michigan

Common Name	Scientific Name	Habitat(s)[1]	Special Status		
			Region 3 Conservation Priorities	Regional Forester Sensitive	Michigan Special Animal
Painted Turtle	*Chrysemys picta*	Ephemeral wetlands, permanent wetlands, rivers and streams, grasslands and savannas, agricultural areas			
Eastern Spiny Softshell	*Trionyx spiniferus*	Rivers and lakes with sand or mud bars			
Chorus Frog	*Pseudacris triseriata*	Permanent wetlands, grasslands and savannas			✓
Northern Spring Peeper	*Pseudacris crucifer crucifer*	Permanent wetlands, forests, grasslands and savannas			
Eastern Gray Treefrog	*Hyla versicolor*	Ephemeral wetlands, permanent wetlands, forests			
Cope's Gray Treefrog	*Hyla chrysoscelis*	Ephemeral wetlands, permanent wetlands, forests			
Blanchard's Cricket Frog	*Acris crepitans*	Riparian grasslands, swamps, boggy meadows		✓	✓
Green Frog	*Rana clamitans melanota*	Ephemeral wetlands, permanent wetlands, forests, grasslands and savannas			
Bull Frog	*Rana catesbeiana*	Lakes, ponds, bogs, and slow moving streams			
Northern Leopard Frog	*Rana pipiens*	Ephemeral wetlands, permanent wetlands, forests, grasslands and savannas			
Pickerel Frog	*Rana palustris*	Riparian grasslands, bogs, and rocky ravines			
Wood Frog	*Rana sylvatica*	Permanent wetlands, forests			
Eastern American Toad	*Bufo americanus americanus*	Ephemeral wetlands, permanent wetlands, rivers and streams, forests, grasslands and savannas, caves and springs, agricultural areas, urban areas			
Fowler's Toad	*Bufo woodhousei*	Sandy areas, and shorelines			
Mudpuppy	*Necturus maculosus maculosus*	Ephemeral wetlands, agricultural areas			

Possible Herptofaunal Species of Kirtland's Warbler WMA Based on Distribution Patterns in Michigan

Common Name	Scientific Name	Habitat(s)[1]	Special Status		
			Region 3 Conservation Priorities	Regional Forester Sensitive	Michigan Special Animal
Blue Spotted Salamander	*Ambystoma laterale*	Ephemeral wetlands, permanent wetlands, forests, grasslands and savannas			
Spotted Salamander	*Ambystoma maculatum*	Ephemeral wetlands, permanent wetlands, forests			
Eastern Tiger Salamander	*Ambystoma tigrinum tigrinum*	Ephemeral wetlands, permanent wetlands, forests, grasslands and savannas, agricultural areas			
Eastern Newt	*Notophthalmus viridescens*	Ephemeral wetlands, permanent wetlands, forests			
Red-backed Salamander	*Plethodon cinereus*	Forests			
Four-toed Salamander	*Hemidactylium scutatum*	Ephemeral wetlands, permanent wetlands, forests		✓	

1. *Habitat information obtained from: Conant (1975).*

Appendix D: Compliance Requirements

Compliance Requirements

Rivers and Harbor Act (1899) (33 U.S.C. 403)

Section 10 of this Act requires the authorization by the U.S. Army Corps of Engineers prior to any work in, on, over, or under a navigable water of the United States.

Antiquities Act of 1906. 16 U.S.C. 431 et seq.

Authorizes the scientific investigation of antiquities on Federal land and provides penalties for unauthorized removal of objects taken or collected without a permit.

Migratory Bird Treaty Act, 16 U.S.C. 703 et seq.

Designates the protection of migratory birds as a Federal responsibility. This Act enables the setting of seasons, and other regulations including the closing of areas, Federal or non Federal, to the hunting of migratory birds.

Migratory Bird Conservation Act, 16 U.S.C. 715 et seq.

Establishes procedures for acquisition by purchase, rental, or gift of areas approved by the Migratory Bird Conservation Commission.

Fish and Wildlife Coordination Act 16 U.S.C. 661 et seq. (1934)

Requires that the Fish and Wildlife Service and State fish and wildlife agencies be consulted whenever water is to be impounded, diverted or modified under a Federal permit or license. The Service and State agency recommend measures to prevent the loss of biological resources, or to mitigate or compensate for the damage. The project proponent must take biological resource values into account and adopt justifiable protection measures to obtain maximum overall project benefits. A 1958 amendment added provisions to recognize the vital contribution of wildlife resources to the Nation and to require equal consideration and coordination of wildlife conservation with other water resources development programs. It also authorized the Secretary of Interior to provide public fishing areas and accept donations of lands and funds.

Migratory Bird Hunting Stamp Act. Also known as the Duck Stamp Act, 16 U.S.C. 718 et seq. (1934)

Requires every waterfowl hunter 16 years of age or older to carry a stamp and earmarks proceeds of the Duck Stamps to buy or lease waterfowl habitat. A 1958 amendment authorizes the acquisition of small wetland and pothole areas to be designated as 'Waterfowl Production Areas,' which may be acquired without the limitations and requirements of the Migratory Bird Conservation Act.

Historic Sites, Buildings and Antiquities Act. Also known as the Historic Sites Act of 1935, 16 U.S.C. 461 et seq.

Declares it a national policy to preserve historic sites and objects of national significance, including those located on refuges. Provides procedures for designation, acquisition, administration, and protection of such sites.

Refuge Revenue Sharing Act, 16 U.S.C. 715s (1935)

Requires revenue sharing provisions to all fee-title ownerships that are administered solely or primarily by the Secretary through the Service.

Transfer of Certain Real Property for Wildlife Conservation Purposes Act, 16 U.S.C. 667b-667d (1948)

Provides that upon a determination by the Administrator of the General Services Administration, real property no longer needed by a Federal agency can be transferred without reimbursement to the Secretary of Interior if the land has particular value for migratory birds, or to a State agency for other wildlife conservation purposes.

Federal Records Act of 1950, 44 U.S.C. 31

Directs the preservation of evidence of the government's organization, functions, policies, decisions, operations, and activities, as well as basic historical and other information.

Fish and Wildlife Act of 1956, 16 U.S.C. 742a et seq.

Established a comprehensive national fish and wildlife policy and broadened the authority for acquisition and development of refuges.

Refuge Recreation Act, 16 U.S.C. 460k et seq. (1962)

Allows the use of refuges for recreation when such uses are compatible with the refuge's primary purposes and when sufficient funds are available to manage the uses.

Wilderness Act of 1964, 16 U.S.C. 1131 et seq.

Directed the Secretary of Interior, within 10 years, to review every roadless area of 5,000 or more acres and every roadless island (regardless of size) within National Wildlife Refuge and National Park Systems and to recommend to the President the suitability of each such area or island for inclusion in the National Wilderness Preservation System, with final decisions made by Congress. The Secretary of Agriculture was directed to study and recommend suitable areas in the National Forest System.

Land and Water Conservation Fund Act of 1965, 16 U.S.C. 460 et seq.

Uses the receipts from the sale of surplus Federal land, outer continental shelf oil and gas sales, and other sources for land acquisition under several authorities.

National Wildlife Refuge System Administration Act of 1966, 16 U.S.C. 668dd, 668ee

Defines the National Wildlife Refuge System and authorizes the Secretary to permit any use of a refuge provided such use is compatible with the major purposes for which the refuge was established. The Refuge Improvement Act clearly defines a unifying mission for the Refuge System; establishes the legitimacy and appropriateness of the six priority public uses (hunting, fishing, wildlife observation and photography, or environmental education and interpretation); establishes a formal process for determining compatibility; established the responsibilities of the Secretary of Interior for managing and protecting the System; and requires a Comprehensive Conservation Plan for each refuge by the year 2012. This Act amended portions of the Refuge Recreation Act and National Wildlife Refuge System Administration Act of 1966.

National Historic Preservation Act, 16 U.S.C. 470 et seq. (1966)

Establishes as policy that the Federal Government is to provide leadership in the preservation of the nation's prehistoric and historic resources. Section 106 requires Federal agencies to consider impacts their undertakings could have on historic properties; Section 110 requires Federal agencies to manage historic properties, e.g., to document historic properties prior to destruction or damage; Section 101 requires Federal agencies to consider Indian tribal values in historic preservation programs, and requires each Federal agency to establish a program leading to inventory of all historic properties on its land.

Architectural Barriers Act of 1968, 42 U.S.C. 4151 et seq.

Requires federally owned, leased, or funded buildings and facilities to be accessible to persons with disabilities.

National Environmental Policy Act of 1969, 42 U.S.C. 4321 et seq.

Requires the disclosure of the environmental impacts of any major Federal action significantly affecting the quality of the human environment.

Uniform Relocation Assistance and Real Property Acquisition Policies Act of 1970, 42 U.S.C. 4601 et seq.

Provides for uniform and equitable treatment of persons who sell their homes, businesses, or farms to the Service. The Act requires that any purchase offer be no less than the fair market value of the property.

Endangered Species Act of 1973, 16 U.S.C. 1531 et seq.

Requires all Federal agencies to carry out programs for the conservation of endangered and threatened species.

Rehabilitation Act of 1973, 29 U.S.C. 701 et seq.

Requires programmatic accessibility in addition to physical accessibility for all facilities and programs funded by the Federal government to ensure that anybody can participate in any program.

Archaeological and Historic Preservation Act 16 U.S.C.469-469c

Directs the preservation of historic and archaeological data in Federal construction projects.

Clean Water Act of 1977, 33 U.S.C. 1251

Requires consultation with the Corps of Engineers (404 permits) for major wetland modifications.

Surface Mining Control and Reclamation Act of 1977, 30 U.S.C. 1201 et seq.

Regulates surface mining activities and reclamation of coal-mined lands. Further regulates the coal industry by designating certain areas as unsuitable for coal mining operations.

Executive Order 11988 (1977)

Each Federal agency shall provide leadership and take action to reduce the risk of flood loss and minimize the impact of floods on human safety, and preserve the natural and beneficial values served by the floodplains.

Executive Order 11990

Executive Order 11990 directs Federal agencies to (1) minimize destruction, loss, or degradation of wetlands and (2) preserve and enhance the natural and beneficial values of wetlands when a practical alternative exists.

Executive Order 12372 (Intergovernmental Review of Federal Programs)

Directs the Service to send copies of the Environmental Assessment to State Planning Agencies for review.

American Indian Religious Freedom Act, 42 U.S.C. 1996, 1996a (1976)

Directs agencies to consult with native traditional religious leaders to determine appropriate policy changes necessary to protect and preserve American Indian religious cultural rights and practices.

Fish and Wildlife Improvement Act of 1978, 16 U.S.C. 742a

Improves the administration of fish and wildlife programs and amends several earlier laws including the Refuge Recreation Act, the National Wildlife Refuge System Administration Act, and the Fish and Wildlife Act of 1956. It authorizes the Secretary to accept gifts and bequests of real and personal property on behalf of the United States. It also authorizes the use of volunteers on Service projects and appropriations to carry out a volunteer program.

Archaeological Resources Protection Act of 1979, 16 U.S.C. 470aa et seq.

Protects materials of archaeological interest from unauthorized removal or destruction and requires Federal managers to develop plans and schedules to locate archaeological resources.

Farmland Protection Policy Act, Public Law 97-98, 7 U.S.C. 4201 (1981)

Minimizes the extent to which Federal programs contribute to the unnecessary and irreversible conversion of farmland to nonagricultural uses.

Emergency Wetlands Resources Act of 1986, 16 U.S.C. 3901 et seq.

Promotes the conservation of migratory waterfowl and offsets or prevents the serious loss of wetlands by the acquisition of wetlands and other essential habitats.

Federal Noxious Weed Act of 1974, 7 U.S.C. 2801 et seq.

Requires the use of integrated management systems to control or contain undesirable plant species, and an interdisciplinary approach with the cooperation of other Federal and State agencies.

Native American Graves Protection and Repatriation Act, 25 U.S.C. 3001 et seq. (1990)

Requires Federal agencies and museums to inventory, determine ownership of, and repatriate cultural items under their control or possession.

Americans with Disabilities Act of 1990, 42 U.S.C. 12101 et seq.

Prohibits discrimination in public accommodations and services.

Executive Order 12898 (1994)

Establishes environmental justice as a Federal government priority and directs all Federal agencies to make environmental justice part of their mission. Environmental justice calls for fair distribution of environmental hazards.

Executive Order 12996 Management and General Public Use of the National Wildlife Refuge System (1996)

Defines the mission, purpose, and priority public uses of the National Wildlife Refuge System. It also presents four principles to guide management of the System.

Executive Order 13007 Indian Sacred Sites (1996)

Directs Federal land management agencies to accommodate access to and ceremonial use of Indian sacred sites by Indian religious practitioners, avoid adversely affecting the physical integrity of such sacred sites, and where appropriate, maintain the confidentiality of sacred sites.

National Wildlife Refuge System Improvement Act of 1997, 16 U.S.C. 668dd

Considered the "Organic Act of the National Wildlife Refuge System. Defines the mission of the System, designates priority wildlife-dependent public uses, and calls for comprehensive refuge planning. Section 6 requires the Service to make a determination of compatibility of existing, new and changing uses of Refuge land; and Section 7 requires the Service to identify and describe the archaeological and cultural values of the refuge.

National Wildlife Refuge System Volunteer and Community Partnership Enhancement Act of 1998, 16 U.S.C. 742a Amends the Fish and Wildlife Act of 1956 to promote volunteer programs and community partnerships for the benefit of national wildlife refuges, and for other purposes.

National Trails System Act, 16 U.S.C. 1241 et seq. (1968)

Assigns responsibility to the Secretary of Interior and thus the Service to protect the historic and recreational values of congressionally designated National Historic Trail sites.

Treasury and General Government Appropriations Act, Pub. L. 106-554, §1(a)(3), Dec. 21, 2000, 114 Stat. 2763, 2763A–125

In December 2002, Congress required federal agencies to publish their own guidelines for ensuring and maximizing the quality, objectivity, utility, and integrity of information that they disseminate to the public (44 U.S.C. 3502). The amended language is included in Section 515(a). The Office of Budget and Management (OMB) directed agencies to develop their own guidelines to address the requirements of the law. The Department of the Interior instructed bureaus to prepare separate guidelines on how they would apply the Act. The U.S. Fish and Wildlife Service has developed "Information Quality Guidelines" to address the law.

Cultural Resources and Historic Preservation

The National Wildlife Refuge System Improvement Act of 1997, Section 6, requires the Service to make a determination of compatibility of existing, new and changing uses of Refuge land; and Section 7 requires the Service to identify and describe the archaeological and cultural values of the refuge.

The National Historic Preservation Act (NHPA), Section 106, requires Federal agencies to consider impacts their undertakings could have on historic properties; Section 110 requires Federal agencies to manage historic properties, e.g., to document historic properties prior to destruction or damage; Section 101 requires Federal agencies consider Indian tribal values in historic preservation programs, and requires each Federal agency to establish a program leading to inventory of all historic properties on its land.

The Archaeological Resources Protection Act of 1979 (ARPA) prohibits unauthorized disturbance of archeological resources on Federal and Indian land; and related matters. Section 10 requires establishing "a program to increase public awareness" of archeological resources. Section 14 requires plans to survey lands and a schedule for surveying lands with "the most scientifically valuable archaeological resources." This Act requires protection of all archeological sites more than 100 years old (not just sites meeting the criteria for the National Register) on Federal land, and requires archeological investigations on Federal land be performed in the public interest by qualified persons.

The Native American Graves Protection and Repatriation Act of 1990 (NAGPRA) imposes responsibilities which may result in serious delays on a project when human remains or other cultural items are encountered in the absence of a plan.

The American Indian Religious Freedom Act (AIRFA) iterates the right of Native Americans to free exercise of traditional religions and use of sacred places.

EO 13007, Indian Sacred Sites (1996), directs Federal agencies to accommodate access to and ceremonial use, to avoid adverse effects and avoid blocking access, and to enter into early consultation.

Appendix E: Appropriate Use Determinations

Appropriate Refuge Uses

The Service's Appropriate Use policy describes the initial decision process a refuge manager follows when first considering whether or not to allow a proposed use on a refuge. The refuge manager must first find a use to be appropriate before undertaking a compatibility review of the use and outlining the stipulations of the use.

This policy clarifies and expands on the compatibility policy (603 FW 2.10D(1)), which describes when refuge managers should deny a proposed use without determining compatibility. If we find a proposed use is not appropriate, we will not allow the use and will not prepare a compatibility determination. By screening out proposed uses not appropriate to the refuge, the refuge manager avoids unnecessary compatibility reviews. By following the process for finding the appropriateness of a use, we strengthen and fulfill the Refuge System mission. Although a refuge use may be both appropriate and compatible, the refuge manager retains the authority to not allow the use or modify the use.

Background for this policy as it applies to Kirtland's Warbler WMA is found in the following statutory authorities:

National Wildlife Refuge System Administration Act of 1966, as amended by the *National Wildlife Refuge System Improvement Act of 1997* (16 U.S.C. 668dd-668ee). This law provides the authority for establishing policies and regulations governing refuge uses, including the authority to prohibit certain harmful activities. The Administration Act does not authorize any particular use, but rather authorizes the Secretary of the Interior to allow uses only when they are compatible. The Improvement Act provides the Refuge System mission and includes specific directives and a clear hierarchy of public uses on the Refuge System.

Refuge Recreation Act of 1962, (16 U.S.C. 460k). This law authorizes the Secretary of the Interior to allow public recreation in areas of the Refuge System when the use is an "appropriate incidental or secondary use."

This policy does not apply to:

■ Situations where reserved rights or legal mandates provide we must allow certain uses.

Refuge Management Activities. Refuge management activities conducted by the Refuge System or a Refuge System-authorized agent are designed to conserve fish, wildlife, and plants and their habitats. These activities are used to fulfill a refuge purpose(s) or the Refuge System mission, and are based on sound professional judgment.

Uses that have been administratively determined to be appropriate are:

■ *Six wildlife-dependent recreational uses.* As defined by the National Wildlife Refuge System Improvement Act of 1997 (Improvement Act), the six wildlife-dependent recreational uses (hunting, fishing, wildlife observation and photography, and environmental education and interpretation) are determined to be appropriate. However, the refuge manager must still determine if these uses are compatible.

■ *Take of fish and wildlife under State regulations.* States have regulations concerning take of wildlife that includes hunting, fishing, and trapping. We consider take of wildlife under such regulations appropriate. However, the refuge manager must determine if the activity is compatible before allowing it on a refuge.

Refuge uses must meet at least one of the following four conditions to be deemed appropriate:

- It is a wildlife-dependent recreational use of a refuge as identified in the Improvement Act.

- It contributes to fulfilling the refuge purpose(s), the Refuge System mission, or goals or objectives described in a refuge management plan approved after the Improvement Act was signed into law.

- The use involves the take of fish and wildlife under State regulations.

- The refuge manager has evaluated the use following the guidelines in this policy and found that it is appropriate. The criteria used by the manager to evaluate appropriateness can be found on each of the appropriate use forms included in this appendix. Also included under this condition are 'specialized uses,' or uses that require specific authorization from the Refuge System, often in the form of a special use permit, letter of authorization, or other permit document. These uses do not include uses already granted by a prior existing right. We make appropriateness findings for specialized uses on a case-by-case basis.

Finding of Appropriateness of a Refuge Use

Refuge Name: ___Kirtland's Warbler Wildlife Management Area_____

Use: __Research_____

This exhibit is not required for wildlife-dependent recreational uses, forms of take regulated by the State, or uses already described in a refuge CCP or step-down management plan approved after October 9, 1997.

Decision Criteria:	YES	NO
(a) Do we have jurisdiction over the use?	X	
(b) Does the use comply with applicable laws and regulations (Federal, State, tribal, and local)?	X	
(c) Is the use consistent with applicable Executive orders and Department and Service policies?	X	
(d) Is the use consistent with public safety?	X	
(e) Is the use consistent with goals and objectives in an approved management plan or other document?	X	
(f) Has an earlier documented analysis not denied the use or is this the first time the use has been proposed?	X	
(g) Is the use manageable within available budget and staff?	X	
(h) Will this be manageable in the future within existing resources?	X	
(i) Does the use contribute to the public's understanding and appreciation of the refuge's natural or cultural resources, or is the use beneficial to the refuge's natural or cultural resources?	X	
(j) Can the use be accommodated without impairing existing wildlife-dependent recreational uses or reducing the potential to provide quality (see section 1.6D. for description), compatible, wildlife-dependent recreation into the future?	X	

Where we do not have jurisdiction over the use ("no" to (a)), there is no need to evaluate it further as we cannot control the use. Uses that are illegal, inconsistent with existing policy, or unsafe ("no" to (b), (c), or (d)) may not be found appropriate. If the answer is "no" to any of the other questions above, we will generally not allow the use.

If indicated, the refuge manager has consulted with State fish and wildlife agencies.   Yes _X_   No ___

When the refuge manager finds the use appropriate based on sound professional judgment, the refuge manager must justify the use in writing on an attached sheet and obtain the refuge supervisor's concurrence.

Based on an overall assessment of these factors, my summary conclusion is that the proposed use is:

Not Appropriate_____   Appropriate_X_

Acting Refuge Manager: _____   Date: 9/8/2009

If found to be Not Appropriate, the refuge supervisor does not need to sign concurrence if the use is a new use.
If an existing use is found Not Appropriate outside the CCP process, the refuge supervisor must sign concurrence.
If found to be Appropriate, the refuge supervisor must sign concurrence.

Refuge Supervisor: _____   Date: 9/10/09

A compatibility determination is required before the use may be allowed.

Appendix F: Compatibility Determinations

COMPATIBILITY DETERMINATION

Use: Hunting

Refuge Name: Kirtland's Warbler Wildlife Management Area (WMA)

Establishing and Acquisition Authorities: Endangered Species Act 16 U.S.C 1531-1543

Refuge Purpose(s): Kirtland's Warbler Wildlife Management Area was established in 1980...
"... to conserve (A) fish or wildlife which are listed as endangered species or threatened species .... or (B) plants ..." 16 U.S.C. § 1534

National Wildlife Refuge System Mission: To administer a national network of lands and waters for the conservation, management, and where appropriate, restoration of fish, wildlife and plant resources and their habitats within the United States for the benefit of present and future generations of Americans.

Description of Use:

What is the use? The use is the hunting of game, an activity conducted by the general public under authority of the National Wildlife Refuge System Improvement Act. Hunting is currently allowed for all game species within the State of Michigan, in accordance with State regulations. However, we estimated that fewer than 200 people hunt on the Kirtland's Warbler WMA. Most hunting is incidental to hunting that occurs on adjacent State and privately owned land. Commonly hunted species include: Ruffed Grouse, American Woodcock, gray squirrel, snowshoe hare, and white-tailed deer.

Where is the use conducted? The Kirtland's Warbler WMA consists of 125 parcels of land located in the counties of Clare, Crawford, Kalkaska, Montmorency, Presque Isle, Ogemaw, Oscoda, and Roscommon, totaling 6,684 acres.

When is the use conducted? Hunting season traditionally runs from mid-September through the end of December for species typically hunted on Kirtland's Warbler WMA. The regular firearm season for white-tailed deer, which is the most popular hunting season in the State, runs from November 15 – 30.

How is the use conducted? Hunting is conducted under regulations promulgated by the State of Michigan.

Why is the use being proposed? Hunting is identified as a priority public use in the National Wildlife Refuge System Improvement Act of 1997 and has traditionally occurred on lands within the Kirtland's WMA without adverse impacts to the purpose for which the Area was established. The hunt program is administered in accordance with sound wildlife management principles and the utmost concern for public safety.

Availability of Resources: Approximately $5,000 is required annually to administer the hunting program on the Kirtland's WMA. This cost is for Law Enforcement patrol to insure compliance with hunting regulations. Based on a review of the current Refuge budget, there is enough funding to ensure administration of this program is compatible with the purpose for which Kirtland's Warbler WMA was established.

Anticipated Impacts of the Use: Hunting has not caused any adverse impacts to the WMA, its habitats, visitors or wildlife. Concerns over impacts to Kirtland's Warblers, other non-target wildlife and visitors are minimized by the seasonality of the hunts. Hunting occurs after the nesting season and after Kirtland's Warblers and many other non-target wildlife have migrated south. It is also the time when visitation is at its lowest. Hunters are required to follow all Michigan State hunting regulations and law enforcement patrols are conducted regularly to ensure compliance with regulations. The hunting program follows all applicable laws, regulations and policies; including, Title 50 Code of Federal Regulations, National Wildlife Refuge System Manual, National Wildlife Refuge System goals and objectives. This activity is also compliant with the purpose of the Refuge and the National Wildlife Refuge System Mission. Conducting this program does not alter the Service's ability to meet habitat goals, provides for public safety and supports several primary objectives of the WMA.

Public Review and Comment: This compatibility determination was part of the Draft Kirtland's Warbler Wildlife Management Area Comprehensive Conservation Plan and Environmental Assessment, which was announced in the Federal Register and available for public comment for 30 days.

Determination:

__ Use is not compatible.

 X Use is compatible with the following stipulations.

Stipulations Necessary to Ensure Compatibility: To ensure compatibility with National Wildlife Refuge System and Kirtland's Warbler WMA goals and objectives the activity can only occur under the following stipulations:

1.   State and/or Tribal hunting requirements apply to all hunting on the Kirtland's Warbler WMA.

2.   Annually review all hunting activities and operations to ensure compliance with all applicable laws, regulations and policies.

Justification: This use has been determined compatible provided the above stipulations are implemented. This use is being permitted as it is a priority public use and will not diminish the primary purposes of the WMA. This use will meet the mission of the National Wildlife Refuge System by providing renewable resources for the benefit of the American public while conserving fish, wildlife and plant resources on these lands.

Signature: _____ 9/8/2009

Acting Refuge Manager   Date

Concurrence: _____ 9/11/2009

ActingRegional Chief   Date

Mandatory 10 or 15 year Re-evaluation Date: 2024

COMPATIBILITY DETERMINATION

Use: Environmental Education and Interpretation, Wildlife Observation, and Photography (including means of access)

Refuge Name: Kirtland's Warbler Wildlife Management Area

Establishing and Acquisition Authorities: Endangered Species Act 16 U.S.C 1531-1543

Refuge Purpose(s): Kirtland's Warbler Wildlife Management Area was established in 1980...
"... to conserve (A) fish or wildlife which are listed as endangered species or threatened species .... or (B) plants ..." 16 U.S.C. § 1534

National Wildlife Refuge System Mission: To administer a national network of lands and waters for the conservation, management, and where appropriate, restoration of fish, wildlife and plant resources and their habitats within the United States for the benefit of present and future generations of Americans.

Description of Use:

What is the use? Provide opportunities for the public to observe and photograph wildlife and engage in environmental interpretation and education. Environmental education consists of public outreach and onsite activities conducted by refuge staff, volunteers, teachers, and university professors. Interpretation occurs in less formal activities with refuge staff and volunteers or through exhibits, signs, and brochures. Under the National Wildlife Refuge System Improvement Act of 1997, environmental education, interpretation, wildlife observation and photography are priority public uses.

Where is the use conducted? These activities are most likely to take place in or near areas where Kirtland's Warblers are nesting; specifically jack-pine habitat 5-20 years of age. Access would be along county roads by motorized vehicle, bicycle and on foot.

When is the use conducted? Visitation to the Kirtland's Warbler WMA is highest during the nesting season (May 15 – July 15).

How is the use conducted? The U.S. Fish and Wildlife Service, with assistance from the Michigan Audubon Society and the U.S. Forest Service, provide daily tours to observe and photograph Kirtland's Warblers. These tours typically begin during the week of May 15 and end the first week in July. The Michigan Department of Natural Resources also provides tours during the Kirtland's Warbler Festival which is hosted annually by the Kirtland Community College. All participants are given an interpretive brochure and the staff, who serve as guides, provide environmental education. Interpretive signs are also used to clarify why nesting areas are closed and explain management of the jack-pine ecosystem for Kirtland's Warblers. Nearly 1,500 people participate in the tours annually. These tours may or may not visit Kirtland's Warbler WMA lands, depending upon where birds can be easily seen with minimal disturbance.

All wildlife observation and photography activities will be conducted with the Kirtland's Warbler WMA's goals, objectives and management plans as the guiding principles. Activities done under these restrictions allow the Service to accomplish its management and provide for the safety of visitors. Entry on all or portions of individual areas may be temporarily suspended due to unusual or critical conditions affecting land, water, vegetation, wildlife populations, or public safety.

Why is the use being proposed? Environmental education, interpretation, wildlife observation and photography are priority public uses on National Wildlife Refuge System lands as identified in the National Wildlife Refuge System Improvement Act of 1997. Allowing access to the Refuge for these activities is consistent with goals of the Kirtland's Warbler WMA and the National Wildlife Refuge System.

Availability of Resources: All of the cost associated with providing environmental education and interpretation, wildlife observation and photography are borne by other government agencies and non-government organizations.

Anticipated Impacts of the Use: Environmental education and interpretation and/or wildlife observation and photography tours are designed to minimize disturbance to wildlife. Kirtland's Warblers quickly become accustom to vehicles along designated routes and when people get out of vehicles to set up cameras, the impact is negligible and temporary. People who do attempt to locate birds on their own are restricted to county roads. Overall, the disturbance is limited to a small portion of the entire Kirtland's Warbler WMA.

Environmental education and interpretation, wildlife observation and photography are priority public uses listed in the National Wildlife Refuge System Improvement Act. By facilitating these activities on the Kirtland's Warbler WMA, we will increase visitors' knowledge and appreciation of endangered species, which will foster public stewardship of fish and wildlife and their habitats. Increased public stewardship will lead to support for Service activities and further the mission of the National Wildlife Refuge System.

Public Review and Comment: This compatibility determination was part of the Draft Kirtland's Warbler Wildlife Management Area Comprehensive Conservation Plan and Environmental Assessment, which was announced in the Federal Register and available for public comment for 30 days.

Determination:

_____ Use is not compatible.

__X__ Use is compatible with the following stipulations.

Stipulations Necessary to Ensure Compatibility: To ensure compatibility with National Wildlife Refuge System and Kirtland's Warbler WMA goals and objectives, environmental education, interpretation, wildlife observation and photography can only occur under the following stipulation:

1.   Visitors must adhere to seasonal closures issued by the Director of the Michigan Department of Natural Resources

Justification: This use has been determined compatible provided the above stipulations are implemented. It promotes public stewardship of natural resources and helps the Service meet its goals and objectives. It does not materially interfere with or detract from the Service's ability to meet the mission of the National Wildlife Refuge System.

The activities follow all applicable laws, regulations and policies; including Migratory Bird Conservation Act, Title 50 Code of Federal Regulations, National Wildlife Refuge System Manual, National Wildlife Refuge System goals and objectives. These activities are compliant with the purpose of the Kirtland's Warbler WMA and the National Wildlife Refuge System Mission. Operating this activity does not alter the Service's ability to meet habitat goals and it helps support several of the primary objectives of the National Wildlife Refuge System.

Signature: _____ 9/8/2009 _____

Acting Refuge Manager   Date

Concurrence: _____ 9/11/2009 _____

Acting Regional Chief   Date

Mandatory 10 or 15 year Re-evaluation Date: 2024

COMPATIBILITY DETERMINATION

Use: Research

Refuge Name: Kirtland's Warbler Wildlife Management Area (WMA)

Establishing and Acquisition Authorities: Endangered Species Act 16 U.S.C 1531-1543

Refuge Purpose(s): Kirtland's Warbler Wildlife Management Area was established in 1980...
"... to conserve (A) fish or wildlife which are listed as endangered species or threatened species .... or (B) plants ..." 16 U.S.C. § 1534

National Wildlife System Mission: To administer a national network of lands and waters for the conservation, management, and where appropriate, restoration of fish, wildlife and plant resources and their habitats within the United States for the benefit of present and future generations of Americans.

Description of Use:

What is the use? The use is research conducted by academic institutions, government agencies and private conservation organizations. Research projects will focus on better understanding jack-pine ecosystems and Kirtland's Warbler ecology. It will provide information that increases life history information on species of concern and improves adaptive management decisions.

Where is the use conducted? Research activities will occur throughout the Kirtland's Warbler WMA, which consists of 6,684 acres and adjacent state land.

When is the use conducted? Research may occur at all times of the year day or night. However, most research activity occurs during the summer months (May, June, and July) and during daylight hours.

How is the use conducted? Prior to any research being conducted on the Kirtland's Warbler WMA, a research proposal must be approved by the Kirtland's Warbler Recovery Team. Strict guidelines will be placed on research activities and these guidelines will be incorporated into a Special Use Permit that will be issued by the Refuge Manager. Research may be carried out by professors, students, contractors, and agency staff and volunteers.

All research activities will be conducted in accordance with the Kirtland's Warbler Recovery Plan, the Endangered Species Act and the Kirtland's Warbler WMA primary goals, objectives, and habitat management requirements as the guiding principles. Every effort will be made to minimize the impacts of research activities on wildlife and their habitats and avoid conflicts with public use and management activities.

Why is the use being proposed? Research and monitoring information are critical to making sound biological decisions in the restoration and management of ecosystems/landscapes for fish and wildlife communities occurring on national wildlife refuges. It is needed to measure the successes and failures of management efforts. This is an important use with long-term benefits that ensures we have the best information possible upon which to base management decisions.

Availability of Resources: Approximately $5,000 is required annually to administer the research program at the Kirtland's Warbler WMA. Most of the research and monitoring is funded by grants, other government agencies, universities, or conducted by students and volunteers. U.S. Fish and Wildlife staff involvement includes reviewing research proposals, supervising or monitoring research activities, reviewing reports, providing some equipment and vehicles, and occasionally participating in field work. Based on a review of the current Refuge budget, there is enough funding to ensure administration of this program is compatible with the purpose for which the Kirtland's Warbler WMA was established.

Anticipated Impacts of the Use: Disturbance to wildlife and vegetation by researchers could occur through vegetation sampling, capture and handling of wildlife, observation activities, banding, and accessing the study area. It is possible that direct or indirect mortality could result as a byproduct of research activities. However, the overall impact of allowing well designed and properly reviewed research to be conducted by non-Service personnel is likely to have very little impact on wildlife populations. Research conducted in accordance with Special Use Permits will likely have no adverse impacts. Any negative impacts that occur will likely be outweighed by the knowledge gained and subsequent improvement in management of the jack pine ecosystem.

Public Review and Comment: This compatibility determination was part of the Draft Kirtland's Warbler Wildlife Management Area Comprehensive Conservation Plan and Environmental Assessment, which was announced in the Federal Register and available for public comment for 30 days.

Determination:

____ Use is not compatible.

__X__ Use is compatible with the following stipulations.

Stipulations Necessary to Ensure Compatibility: To ensure compatibility with National Wildlife Refuge System and Kirtland's Warbler WMA goals and objectives the activity can only occur under the following stipulations:

1.   Each research proposal is evaluated to insure the least invasive techniques are used, and preference is given to projects that focus on better understanding of jack-pine ecosystems, and Kirtland's Warbler ecology.

2.   Any research that involves the handling of Kirtland's Warblers must be approved by the Kirtland's Warbler Recovery Team.

3.   The Kirtland's Warbler Recovery Team will be kept apprised on all research activities.

4.   Conditions of Special Use Permits must be followed.

Research activities are evaluated annually to ensure that their collective impacts do not compromise the goals or objectives of Kirtland's Warbler WMA.

Justification: This use has been determined compatible provided the above stipulations are implemented. Research and monitoring information is critical to making sound biological decisions in the restoration and management of ecosystems/landscapes for fish and wildlife communities occurring on lands within the National Wildlife Refuges system. It is needed to measure the successes and failures of management efforts. This is an important use with long-term benefits that ensures we have the best information possible upon which to base management decisions.

Signature: _Greg McClellan_ _9/8/2009_
 Acting Refuge Manager   Date

Concurrence: _Tate Wentworth_ _9/11/2009_
 ~~Acting~~ Regional Chief   Date

Mandatory 10 or 15 year Re-evaluation Date: 2019

Appendix G: Bibliography and References Cited

Bibliography and References Cited

Albert, D.A. 1995. Regional Landscape Ecosystems of Michigan, Minnesota, and Wisconsin: A working Map and Classification. USDA Forest Service North Central Forest Experiment Station General Technical Report NC-178.

American Ornithologists' Union Checklist of North American Birds. 2006. American Ornithologists' Union, McLean, VA. http://www.aou.org/checklist/index.php3.

Brewer, R., McPeek, G. A. and Adams Jr., R. J., eds. 1991. The Atlas of Breeding Birds of Michigan. Michigan State University Press, East Lansing, Michigan.

Conant, R. 1975. A Field Guide to Reptiles and Amphibians of Eastern and Central North America. Houghton Mifflin Co., Boston.

Denton, S.R. 1985. Ecological climatic regions and tree distributions in Michigan. Ph.D. dissertation, University of Michigan, Ann Arbor, MI. 321 pp.

Dorr, J. and D.F. Eschman, 1970. Geology of Michigan. Univeristy of Michigan Press. 476 p.

Dufrêne, M., and Legendre, P. 1997. Species assemblages and indicator species: the need for a flexible asymmetrical approach. Ecological Monographs. 67: 345-366.

Ehrlich, P.R., Dobkin, D.S. and Wheye, D. 1988. The Birder's Handbook: A Field Guide to the Natural History of North American Birds. Simon and Schuster Incorporated, New York, New York.

Frehlich, L. 2002. Forest dynamics and disturbance regimes. Cambridge University Press.

Goebel, P. C., McCormick, D. L. and Corace, R. G., III. 2007. Ecological assessment of the USDI Fish and Wildlife Service's Kirtland's Warbler Wildlife Management Area. The School of Environment and Natural Resources, Ohio Agricultural Research and Development Center, The Ohio State University.

Harrington, E. 2006. Small mammals, habitat, and forest restoration at Seney National Wildlife Refuge. Master's Thesis (Natural Resources and Environment), University of Michigan, Ann Arbor, MI.

Holling, C.S. and G.K. Meffe. 1996. Command and control and the pathology of natural resource management. Conservation Biology 10:328-337.

Iverson, L.R., A.M. Prasad, B.J. Hale, and E.K. Sutherland. 1999. Atlas of current and potential future distributions of common trees of the eastern United States. U. S. Forest Service, Northeastern Research Station, General Technical Report NE-265.

Jenness Random Point Generator v. 1.3. 2005. Jenness Enterprises, Flagstaff, AZ. http://www.jennessent.com/arcview/random_points.htm.

Kashian, D. M, B. V. Barnes, and W. S. Walker. 2003. Landscape ecosystems of northern lower Michigan and the occurrence and management of the Kirtland's Warbler. Forest Science 49:140-159.

Kirtland's Warbler Recovery Plan. 1985. Kirtland's Warbler Recovery Team, Cadillac, Michigan.

Kurta, A. 2001. Mammals of the Great Lakes Region. University of Michigan Press, Ann Arbor.

Lambeck, R.J. 1997. Focal species: a multi-species umbrella for nature conservation. Conservation Biology 11:849-856.

Matthews, S., R. O'Connor, L.R. Iverson, and A.M. Prasad. 2004. Atlas of climate change effects in 150 bird species of the Eastern United States. GTR-NE-318. USDA Forest Service,

Northeastern Research Station. Newtown Square, PA. 340pp. http://www.treesearch.fs.fed.us/pubs/7514

McCune, B., and Mefford, M.J. 1995. PC-ORD, multivariate analysis of ecological data, version 3.0. MjM Software Design, Gleneden Beach, Oregon.

Michigan Department of Natural Resources. 2005. Michigan Wildlife Action Plan. Lansing, Michigan.

Michigan Geographic Data Library. 2006. Michigan Department of Information Technology, Lansing, MI. http://www.mcgi.state.mi.us/mgdl/.

Mielke, P.W. 1984. Meteorological applications of permutation techniques based on distance functions. Pages 813-830, In P.R. Krishnaiah and P.K. Sen (eds.), Handbook of Statistics, Vol. 4. Elsevier Science Publishers.

Muladore, J., S. Pendergrass and R. Schillo. 2006. Conservation planning for the Grayling subdistrict of Michigan. M.S. project, School of Natural Resources and Environment, University of Michigan, Ann Arbor.

National Audubon Society. 2009. (http://www.audubon.org/bird/iba/michigan)

Noss, R. F. and J. M. Scott. 1997. Ecosystem protection and restoration: the core of ecosystem management. Pages 239-264 in M. A. Boyce and A. W. Haney, eds. Ecosystem management: concepts and methods. Yale University Press, New Haven, Conneticut.

Partners In Flight Species Assessment Database. 2006. Rocky Mountain Bird Observatory, Fort Collins, CO. http://www.rmbo.org/pif/pifdb.html.

Prasad, A.M., L.R. Iverson, S. Matthews, M. Peters. 2007-/ongoing. A Climate Change Atlas for 134 Forest Tree Species of the Eastern United States [database]. http://www.nrs.fs.fed.us/atlas/tree Northern Research Station, Forest Service, Delaware, Ohio

Price, J. 2000. Modeling the potential impacts of climate change on the summer distributions of Michigan's nongame birds. Michigan Birds and Natural History 7: 3-11.

Probst, J. R. 1988. Kirtland's Warbler breeding biology and habitat management. In: Integrating Forest Management for Wildlife and Fish. USDA Forest Service General Technical Report, NC-122.

Probst, J. R. and Weinrich, J. 1993. Relating Kirtland's Warbler population to changing landscape composition and structure. Landscape Ecol. 8:257–271.

Probst, J.R., Donner, D.M., Bocettii, C.I., and Sjogren, S. 2003. Population increase in Kirtland's warbler and summer range expansion to Wisconsin and Michigan's Upper Peninsula. Oryx. 37:365-373.

Ralph, J.C., Geupel, G.R., Pyle, P., Martin, T.E. and DeSante, D.F. 1993. Handbook of Field Methods for Monitoring Landbirds. Gen. Tech. Rep. PSW-GTR-144. Pacific Southwest Research Station, Forest Service, U.S. Department of Agriculture, Albany, California.

Root, T. L. and Schneider, S. H. 1995. Ecology and climate: research strategies and implications. Science 269:334-339.

Root, T.L., J.T. Price, K.R. Hall, S.H. Schneider, C. Rosenzweig, and J.A. Pounds. 2003.

Fingerprints of global warming on wild animals and plants. Nature 421:57-60.

Sallabanks, R. and E.B. Arnett. 2005. Accomodating birds in managed forests in North America: a review of bird-forestry relationships. USDA Forest Service PSW-GTR-191.

Seymour, R.S. and M.L. Hunter, Jr. 1999. Principles of Ecological Forestry. Ch. 2 (p. 22-61) In: Managing Biodiversity in Forest Ecosystems. M.L. Hunter, Jr., editor. Cambridge Univ. Press. 698 p.

Simberloff, D. 1997. Flagships, umbrellas, and keystones: is single species management passé in the landscape era. Biological Conservation 83:247-257.

Stevenson, I.R. and D.M. Bryant. 2000. Climate change and constraints on breeding. Nature 406:366-367.

ter Braak, C. J .F. and Šmilauer, P. 1997. Canoco for Windows version 4.02. Centre for Biometry. Wageningen, Netherlands.

The Nature Conservancy. 2000. Toward a New Conservation Vision for the Great Lakes Region: A Second Iteration. The Nature Conservancy. Chicago, Illinois. 44 pages.

United States Census Bureau, 2005. http://www.census.gov/popest/estimates.php

USFWS Conservation Library. 2002. Fish & Wildlife Resources Conservation Priorities – Region 3 (v. 2.0). U.S. Fish & Wildlife Service, Washington DC. http://library.fws.gov/pubs3/priorities02.pdf.

Walker, W. S., B. V. Barnes, and D. M. Kashian. 2003. Landscape ecosystems of the Mack Lake Burn, northern lower Michigan, and the occurrence of the Kirtland's Warbler. Forest Science 49:119-139.

Walkinshaw, L. 1972. Kirtland's Warbler: The Natural History of an Endangered Species. Wayne State University Press. 207p.

Appendix H: List of Preparers

List of Preparers

Refuge Staff:

- Tracy Casselman, Refuge Manager
- Greg Corace, Forester

Regional Office Staff:

- Gary Muehlenhardt, Wildlife Biologist/Refuge Planner, Region 3, USFWS
- Gabriel DeAlessio, Biologist-GIS, Region 3, USFWS
- John Dobrovolny, Regional Historian, Region 3, USFWS (retired)
- Jane Hodgins, Technical Writer/Editor, Region 3, USFWS

Appendix I: Mailing List

Mailing List

The following is a list of government offices, private organizations, and individuals who will receive notice of the availability of this CCP.

Federal Officials

- U.S. Senator Debbie Stabenow
- U.S. Senator Carl Levin
- U.S. Representative Dave Camp
- U.S. Representative Bart Stupak

Federal Agencies

- USDA/Natural Resource Conservation Service
- USDA/Forest Service, Hiawatha National Forest
- USDI/Fish and Wildlife Service, Albuquerque, New Mexico; Anchorage, Alaska; Atlanta, Georgia; Denver, Colorado; Fort Snelling, Minnesota; Hadley, Massachusetts; Portland, Oregon; Sacramento, California; Washington, D.C.
- USDI/East Lansing Private Lands Office; East Lansing Field Office; Alpena Fishery Resources Office; Ann Arbor Law Enforcement Field Office; Great Lakes Science Center, Biological Resources Division, USGS
- USEPA, Great Lakes National Program Office, Chicago, Illinois

Federal and State Officials

- Governor Jennifer Granholm
- U.S. Senator Carl Levin
- U.S. Senator Debbie Stabenow
- U.S. Rep. Bart Stupak
- U.S. Rep. Dave Camp
- State Sen. Michelle McManus
- State Sen. Tony Stamas
- State Sen. Jason Allen
- State Rep. Matthew Gillard
- State Rep. Dale Sheltrown
- State Rep. Tim Moore

- State Rep. Howard Walker

State Agencies

- Director, Michigan Department of Natural Resources
- Area Managers and Biologists, Michigan DNR
- State Historic Preservation Officer, Lansing, Michigan

City/County/Local Governments

- City of Gaylord
- City of Grayling
- Clare County
- Crawford County
- Kalkaska County
- Montmorency County
- Oscoda County
- Ogemaw County
- Presque Isle County
- Roscommon County

Libraries

- Libraries within the eight county region

Organizations

- The Nature Conservancy
- National Audubon Society
- Conservation Fund
- Michigan United Conservation Clubs
- Wildlife Management Institute
- Great Lakes Commission
- Wildlife Management Institute
- PEER Refuge Keeper
- The Wilderness Society, Washington, D.C.
- National Wildlife Federation, Ann Arbor, Michigan
- The Conservation Fund, Arlington, Virginia

Media

- Local Radio and TV Stations; Refuge Media Contacts
- Detroit News
- Detroit Free Press
- Michigan Radio News

Federally-recognized Tribes and Historical Societies

- Michigan State Historic Preservation Officer
- Michigan Office of the State Archeologist
- The Grand Traverse Band of Ottawa and Chippewa Indians
- Michigan Anishinabe Cultural Protection and Repatriation Alliance (Ojibwa)
- The Advisory Council on Historic Preservation

Individuals

- Individuals who participated in open houses, sent written comments, or requested to be on the mailing list.